Effective Schooling for Pupils with Emotional and Behavioural Difficulties

Ted Cole, John Visser
and Graham Upton

David Fulton Publishers
London

David Fulton Publishers Ltd
Ormond House, 26–27 Boswell Street, London WC1N 3JD

First published in Great Britain by David Fulton Publishers 1998

Note: The right of Ted Cole, John Visser and Graham Upton to be identified as the editor of this work has been asserted by them in accordance with the Copyright, Designs and Patents Act 1988.

Copyright © Ted Cole, John Visser and Graham Upton 1998

British Library Cataloguing in Publication Data
A catalogue record for this book is available from the British Library

ISBN 1–85346–544–5

Typeset by Textype Typesetters Ltd, Cambridge
Printed in Great Britain by BPC Books and Journals Ltd, Exeter

Contents

Chapter 1

Introduction

Why do some children with emotional and behavioural difficulties (EBD) settle in some special schools, conform to rules, re-engage in education and acquire nationally-accredited certificates? Yet other special schools struggle to manage pupil behaviour, find it difficult or deem it inappropriate to offer a broad curriculum to a similar clientele and are identified by OFSTED inspectors as 'failing' or having 'serious weaknesses'. What makes the difference between proficient and ostensibly poor provision for the eleven to twelve thousand pupils who are estimated to attend the approximately 280 special schools which are designated as being for pupils with EBD (Visser and Cole 1996)? This last question has been considered by educationalists such as Cooper (1993) and by HMI (Bull 1995, OFSTED 1995a) for some years. It was also a concern of the Audit Commission (1992) in its review of special education.

The present book provides some further answers to this question and reflects on the nature of effectiveness in relation to pupils with emotional and behavioural difficulties. It is based upon research undertaken by the authors during 1996/97. This period was characterised by a number of schools for children with EBD failing OFSTED inspections and the closure of some long-established schools. HMCI (OFSTED 1997) expressed concern over the number of special schools, particularly those for pupils with EBD which were being placed in special measures, a problem which was significant because ostensibly the need for effective provision for pupils with EBD was increasing as a result of:

- rising exclusion rates from the mainstream (Parsons 1995, Blyth and Milner 1996);
- the poor educational performance of pupil referral units (OFSTED 1995e);
- international experience showing the difficulties of including pupils with EBD in mainstream schools (MacMillan *et al.* 1996, Bradshaw 1997).

1

But not only was the research therefore timely but it also constitutes the widest trawl of front-line opinion by a non-governmental body since the Schools Council Project (Dawson 1980, Wilson and Evans 1980).

The first task facing the authors was to identify and quantify the numbers of pupils and where they were placed as this was largely unknown (Visser and Cole 1996). Having established this, the opinions held by the senior staff in special schools for children deemed EBD were surveyed. Fifty-five per cent of all the EBD schools in England completed and returned a detailed twelve-page questionnaire; many schools returned additional questionnaires on child care arrangements and reactions to the 1989 Children Act. At the same time over 80 OFSTED reports on schools for the EBD were analysed and then during1997 two of the authors visited special schools believed to be exemplars of good practice. Visits were also made to schools identified as having serious weaknesses and one which had been deemed to be failing by OFSTED.

In the chapters which follow we provide our analysis of this data base together with a synthesis of previous literature and the views of the staff with whom we have communicated during the project. Our purpose in doing this is to:

- aid understanding of the nature of effective work with children with EBD;
- increase appreciation of the difficulties and pressures of achieving, and then sustaining, good practice;
- celebrate often unsung success;
- provide pointers for mainstream schools to how they might meet the needs of pupils with EBD.

The book looks at the who, the what, the where and the how of effective provision for pupils with EBD in special schools. Having established the historical and theoretical context in Chapter 2, the people involved are discussed – students and their families in Chapter 3, and the staff working with them in Chapter 4. Before proceeding to the programmes provided for, and by, them, we reflect upon the nature of leadership and some aspects of the management task in Chapter 5. In particular, we consider the survey's findings in relation to recent alterations to the legal framework, in particular local management of special schools, the OFSTED inspection process and the 1989 Children Act.

The arguments developed in Chapter 6 are based on the beliefs that the curriculum should be viewed as 'all the learning which is planned and guided by the school, whether it is carried on in groups or individually, inside or outside the school' (Kerr 1968, p. 16), and that learning experiences should be designed to aid the pupils' social and emotional as well as educational development. Much of this will take place in the social milieu outside the classroom, particularly in residential schools. To achieve proficiency with children deemed EBD the affective and the cognitive have to be viewed as a seamless garment (Greenhalgh 1994) or to use the terminology of Bernstein (1977) the pursuit of 'expressive' and 'instrumental' goals must proceed hand in hand. Thus, issues common to social and emotional needs as well as to education are discussed before the focus shifts to the constituents of effective educational provision.

In Chapter 7 we turn to physical considerations. Is there an optimum location? What are the important variables of the physical environment which impinge on effectiveness? Then in the final chapter, our findings are drawn together. We consider how the people, the programmes and the places blend to become and remain *proficient*, a word defined in the Concise Oxford Dictionary as 'adept and expert in doing'. Issues relating to how these schools' effectiveness should be measured are raised. How complete or equitable, for example, is the OFSTED perspective on the school for pupils with EBD? Finally, it is suggested that if some 'ordinary' schools were to examine and adopt some of the practice of proficient special schools, they would be able to meet the needs of a greater number of pupils with EBD within the mainstream.

Chapter 2

History, Theory and Effective Practice

An understanding of the history of provision for children now classified as having emotional and behavioural difficulties helps to make sense of government views in the 1990s, modern theoretical perspectives and of our research findings. In this chapter we therefore examine:

1. who the children have been thought to be and which agencies have taken responsibility for them;
2. themes and dilemmas from the past which still have relevance;
3. recent government views and guidance.

Definition and placement

There is a long history of debate and concern about who the children now said to have emotional and behavioural difficulties are and where they are most appropriately placed (Smith and Thomas 1993a). Children now deemed EBD presented problems to society in Victorian times and were receiving help in a range of provision (Cole 1989). Similarly, the word 'maladjusted' was in official use by 1930 and the first LEA schools for the maladjusted were founded in the 1930s even though the term 'maladjusted' only gained official recognition in the regulations which followed the 1944 Education Act. These defined the maladjusted as

> pupils who show evidence of emotional instability or psychological disturbance and require special education treatment in order to effect their personal, social or educational readjustment. (Ministry of Education 1953)

Laslett (1983) commented on the vagueness of this description and in 1955, the Underwood Committee found it necessary to stress that maladjustment should not be equated with bad behaviour, delinquency, oddness or educational subnormality, suggesting that pupils with a wide range of problems were attending the 33 special schools existing at that time or placed in 'ordinary' independent boarding schools (Ministry of Education 1955). They wished to classify the maladjusted as having nervous, habit, behaviour, organic or psychotic disorders or educational and vocational difficulties to allow for careful matching of provision to children's need. But this was rarely to be achieved and most schools for the maladjusted generally dealt with a diverse clientele, many of whose difficulties could be said to be reactions to environmental factors rather than 'within-child' problems requiring medical-leaning 'treatment' (DES 1974, Laslett 1977, Wilson and Evans 1980).

The Senior Medical Officer at the DES was to note in 1974 that only force of circumstance dictated whether a child went to a school for the maladjusted or to Community Homes with Education (CHEs). The 1963 Children and Young Persons' Act (Hyland 1993) had restated that truants and 'at risk' or 'problem children' (often it was girls who fell into these latter categories) not convicted of crimes could be placed in the Home Office Approved Schools, which after the 1969 Children and Young Persons' Act evolved into Social Service CHEs. In fact, dating back to the work of the Royal Philanthropic Society in the 1790s, the precursors of children with EBD would seem to have been taken under the wing of any one of four government departments – welfare, juvenile justice, education or health. Whether the problem child was cared for, punished, educated or treated was often dependent on which individuals in which agency happened to pick up the case (Hyland 1993, Malek in Grimshaw with Berridge 1994) and a child's placement has often depended on where vacancies were when the child was perceived to have reached crisis point or when funding became available.

Laslett (1983) was right to comment that 'maladjustment' was 'a kind of catch-all for children showing a wide range of behaviour and learning difficulties' (p. 6). While the maladjusted were conceptualised as a separate group, in fact, many children thus labelled could equally have been described as socially deprived, disruptive, disaffected, delinquent, mentally ill or mentally deficient. These were certainly descriptors applied to many children placed in schools for the maladjusted. Conversely, children who might be seen as genuinely maladjusted, have been placed in Home Office, Health or Welfare provisions; or, from the 1970s, in units designed primarily for the so called 'disruptive'.

Where to look for 'the lessons of history'

Echoing the haphazard ascertainment and placement of children, teaching and care staff have moved across the sectors, taking their beliefs and practices with them. Professionals came to work in boarding schools for the maladjusted after experience in child care establishments in the aftermath of the Second World War (Bridgeland 1971). Others later transferred from schools for the maladjusted to the CHE sector (Wills 1971), while many teaching and care staff moved in the opposite direction. Some voluntary agencies such as the National Children's Home and Barnardos long straddled the divide between social work and education and with the disappearance of Approved Schools after the 1969 Children and Young Persons' Act, whole institutions transferred from one sector to another. For example, St Edwards School, Hampshire, moved from being an Approved School to a residential school for pupils with emotional and behavioural difficulties. Other senior staff in CHEs (for example, the founders of the Hesley Hall group of schools) started new schools for pupils with EBD.

In sum, it is not possible to restrict any historical search for good practice to a study of special schools. Nor should we focus exclusively on those early well-known schools which espoused a psychotherapeutic model. Shaw (1965), Lennhoff (1968) and Wills (1960, 1971) all wrote persuasive accounts of their work but significantly they were not qualified teachers and glimpses of the contrasting views of other early workers can be seen, for example, in Bridgeland (1971). The Underwood Report (Ministry of Education 1955) also raised questions about the medical and psychotherapeutic domination of early provision and alluded to the social origins and the situation-specific nature of much challenging behaviour. It is therefore important to look at the ideas and experiences of Home Office and child care sectors whose shadow falls powerfully on the care systems of schools for pupils with EBD in the 1990s.

Our view of the origins of today's special schools is summarised in Table 2.1 which illustrates the range of provision that has been made over the last two centuries for children who today might be considered EBD. The expanding and contracting lines highlight the expansions and contractions in provision which have resulted from different government policies.

From 'perishing classes' to the maladjusted c.1850–1950

Listed below are themes and questions which emerge from historical sources for the century preceding the Underwood Report (Cole 1989).

- Should pupils' perceived problems be viewed as stemming from nature or nurture?

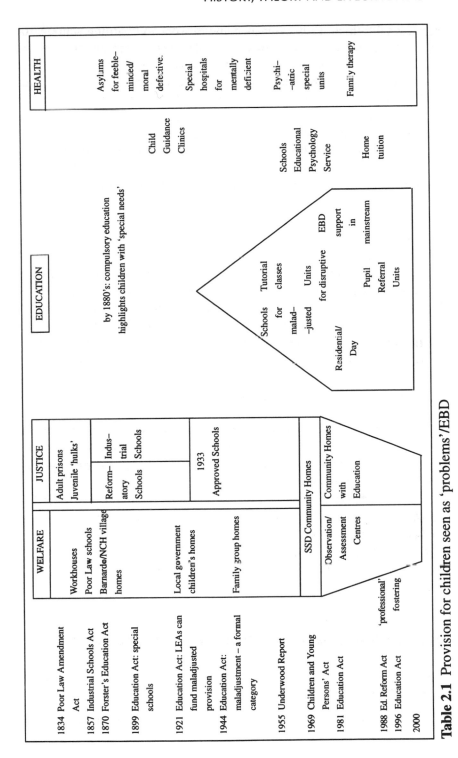

Table 2.1 Provision for children seen as 'problems'/EBD

> If the children of the slums can be removed from their surroundings early enough, and can be kept sufficiently long under training, heredity counts for little, environment counts for everything. (Thomas Barnardo in Heywood 1978, p. 52)

- What is the role of poverty/family influences in behaviour causation?
- Should children be 'rescued' from their families by residential placement or should staff work with the parents while children attend day units/schools (e.g. Victorian 'feeding' or 'truant schools' in the 1880s or Leicester LEA's day school for 'nervous or difficult' children in the 1930s)?
- The need to balance discipline and child-centred care. Many Reformatory and Industrial Schools (RIs) succumbed to an institutionalised and punitive regime which did little to address emotional needs. Mary Carpenter in 1851, for example, pleaded for approaches which 'touch the inner spirit' of the child from what she described as 'the perishing and dangerous classes', and in the 1870s Barnardo started 'ivy clad cottages' to be presided over by housemothers (see Heywood 1978), while Homer Lane and A. S. Neill had experimented with democratic, liberal regimes well before 1925 (Bridgeland 1971).
- The value of routines and reward systems but fears about institutionalisation. The first Inspector of Industrial Schools, Sydney Turner, was well aware of these issues in the mid-nineteenth century (Bridgeland 1971, Carlebach 1967) and Barnardo banned uniforms for the girls in his cottage homes while 'anything approaching institutionalism' was 'scrupulously avoided' (Heywood 1978, p. 52). Aichhorn (1951) was to write in the 1920s, 'We must give the pupils experiences which fit them for life outside and not for the artificial life of an institution' (p. 151).
- The potential of residential schooling to reduce juvenile delinquency. In contrast to the 1970s, in most periods before the War, there were very low rates of recidivism amongst leavers from RIs.
- Lack of money affects quality of education and care and employment of suitable staff. Producing saleable goods sometimes replaced worthwhile trade training in Victorian RIs (Hyland 1993). The gardener, for example, was paid the same as the school mistress and 50 per cent more than the matron of a late nineteenth century girls' industrial school and matron was allowed only one day off every two months (Stanley 1977).
- Can inner-city sites be developed to meet the needs of problem

children? Managers of nineteenth century industrial schools situated in towns found it beneficial to move to rural or semi-rural settings for health reasons and for access to bigger and better sites (Cole 1989).

- The value of education as therapy was seen in some early schools for the maladjusted.

    The school itself was a therapeutic situation and I would guess that about three-quarters of the children received no other form of therapy. (An early headteacher of the Oxford LEA day school, founded 1939. In Bridgeland 1971, p. 298)

- The value of individual work planning, pupils marking their own work, peer tutoring and play, seen at the pre-war Leicester day school for maladjusted (Bridgeland 1971).

The Underwood era 1950–1975

The 1944 Education Act required LEAs to ascertain all children in need of special educational treatment and to make suitable provision according to each child's age, aptitude and ability. In the case of the maladjusted the purpose was 'to effect their personal, social or educational readjustment' (Ministry of Education 1953). Laslett (1983) argued that this particular ordering of the words signified the dominance of a so-called 'medical model' in this period. But was this the case? Only the word treatment has a medical connotation and even this, as Wilson and Evans (1980) stress, and the Oxford Shorter English Dictionary makes plain, can have much wider non-medical meanings. Is it also noteworthy that the familiar acronym of recent decades, 'PSE', receives an early airing?

While doctors played an important part in ascertaining pupils as maladjusted until the 1970s, and child guidance clinics, staffed by psychiatrists, psychiatric social workers as well as psychologists expanded during that period, the evidence that they dominated the actual delivery of care and education programmes rests on uncertain foundations, given our present state of knowledge. Medically-oriented staff certainly influenced what was on offer in some schools, but it is uncertain whether this was a national or a largely London and Home Counties phenomenon. It seems unlikely that the medical model reached significantly into the mainstream schools to which pupils from special hostels went, or some of the 32 early special boarding schools which were founded in the post-war 'country house period' (Ministry of Education 1956), or the 153 'ordinary' boarding schools in which the maladjusted were placed at the time of the Underwood

Report (Ministry of Education 1955). Only limited evidence is offered by Laslett (1983), and Bridgeland (1971, p. 215) records at least one early headteacher who objected to Freudian views and often described doctors and psychiatrists as 'a nutty lot'. Weaver (1968) records that 28 per cent of maladjusted schools offered GCE courses: clearly by the early 1960s at least, some schools for the maladjusted were taking education very seriously – although Weaver also notes that many headteachers did not view educational timetables as very important and that child guidance staff clearly influenced on many schools.

It is also clear that, post-war, the Ministry of Education encouraged some policies which were social and educational rather than medical. Where possible, maladjusted children were to be helped within their local community, by transfer to different mainstream schools, by the use of foster homes or by living in small hostels and attending local day schools (Ministry of Education 1946). For financial and for philosophical reasons it was hoped that day schools or special classes would be developed, extending pre-war experiments in Leicester and Oxford. In 1950, tutorial classes, the precursors of the small special units of the 1970s, were started in London. Maladjusted children attended these centres for part of the week and their teachers – not medical staff from a Child Guidance Clinic – had time allowed for working with the children's families.

In 1950, the Underwood Committee began a major enquiry (Ministry of Education 1955) into provision for maladjusted children. While it was dominated by doctors there are many comments in its report with a psychosocial and educational ring. It recorded, for example, 'a considerable difference of opinion about the need for psychotherapy' (p. 77) and there are many observations which are similar to views expressed by respondents to our questionnaires in 1996/7.

The Underwood perspective on maladjustment

Maladjustment is not a medical term diagnosing a medical condition. . . . It is a term describing an individual's relation at a particular time to the people and circumstances which make up his environment. (Ministry of Education 1955, p. 22)

Maladjusted children are 'insecure and unhappy, and . . . fail in their personal relationships. Receiving is difficult for them as well as giving, and they appear unable to respond to simple measures of love, comfort and reassurance. At the same time, they are not readily capable of improvement by ordinary discipline'. (p. 22)

Approaches to teaching and care

Initial training for teachers should include the emotional development and needs of children; teachers should have a grasp of the normal before training to work with the maladjusted; it is important that teachers help with care duties in residential schools; the value of play; toleration of 'acting out' in class seen as necessary in London day classes and the need to wait until some disturbed children were 'ready' to tackle conventional education. (pp. 54–5)

The simple fact of receiving individual attention in a small class in an informal non-competitive atmosphere often enables a boy or girl to make progress and this can help in solving a child's emotional problems. (p. 72)

Supervision does not imply that children require to be closely watched all the time; nor would this be conducive to their development. (p. 74)

In our view there is a place both for schools which provide psychotherapy and for those which do not. Much can be done for most maladjusted children through personal relationships in a good environment where they feel that they are accepted. (p. 77)

Curriculum

Some children who are 'bright but not bookish' find that as the work becomes more abstract and formal it does not suit them. They cannot cope with the variety of subjects and with the many changes of teacher. (p. 32)

London County Council say of their day classes, that by giving pupils 'a feeling of progress in mastering the 3 Rs, the resultant satisfaction and release may flow over to help to overcome more fundamental troubles'. (p. 53)

Maintaining links with mainstream schools

Pupils at London part-time special classes, stay on the rolls of their mainstream schools. (p. 55)

Children from hostels attend mainstream schools. (p. 66)

The importance of the personality of the staff

> Much more can be done for a child who is maladjusted by a teacher who is warm-hearted and loving than by one who approaches maladjustment through the abnormal and broods over him as a problem child. (p. 140)

> Experience is a good instructor, and the right qualities of character and personality are essential; no training, however thorough, can be a substitute for them. (p. 122)

The importance of controlling intake

> The art of selection is to find comparable children and the right proportions in which to combine children with different characteristics; as one witness said, running a special school is like mixing a pudding. (p. 76)

Location

> It has often been found better to have the premises of a class quite separate from a school, since school may have unhappy associations for many maladjusted children and since an independent class runs on free lines it is not likely to fit in with the routine of an ordinary school. (p. 55)

> Integration into the local community may be easier to achieve in small towns. (p. 66)

Wanting a proactive and preventative approach involving close working between all relevant professions, the Underwood Report recommended:

- a comprehensive child guidance service involving early intervention and work with the child's family. Child guidance must both 'have roots in the school' and 'yet be closely connected with the school health service and other health services' (p. 41);
- more special classes and day schools to obviate the need for so many residential placements (pp. 53–5).

The Report also highlights tension which persists to this day between staff from, and within, different professions about what constitutes effectiveness. How, for example, should maladjustment be addressed? Some espousing a neo-Freudian or psychodynamic viewpoint, have seen it as a 'within child' mental health issue to be tackled by psychiatry, psychotherapy and counselling, with formal education less important. A variant of this view was the concept of milieu therapy (Bettelheim 1950, Redl and Wineman 1952, 1957, Trieschman *et al.* 1969). Emanating from America but finding a ready audience among some pioneer British workers, this advocated the careful structuring of the residential milieu, providing good quality primary care and some formal counselling by qualified staff. But also important was the creative use of the daily events of staff and children living together to allow informal counselling, described by Redl as the 'life-space interview' (LSI). Whittaker (1981) described this as:

> A set of action-based interview strategies designed to help child-care workers deal with real-life problems of children when and where they occur. Life space refers to the total physical, social, psychological, and cultural 'space' surrounding an individual at any given point in time. (p. 95)

In the 1950s and 1960s, the LSI remained a somewhat alien approach to many teachers and care workers but not at some special schools and residential treatment centres which saw themselves as therapeutic communities; as much as agents of mental health as of special education. The work of Bowlby (1953) on the chronic disturbance which flowed if the bonding between a baby and its mother was disturbed, was also influential in their work. Stressing mothering, regression, primary care and using the daily events of residential community living to repair and develop the incomplete egos of 'frozen' and 'archipelago' children was at the heart, for example, of Dockar-Drysdale's (1968) approach.

Therapeutic communities stressed the need to offer contrasting alternatives to mainstream schools. Sometimes their forms of organisation were very different; often characterised by flattened management hierarchies with informal relationships between staff and pupils, democratic community meetings, a non-punitive and permissive regime with a stress on caring relationships. Although, as Wills (1971) stressed, there was also 'reality confrontation' in which children were made to face up to the consequences of their sometimes unsociable and abnormal behaviours. In some of these schools, conventional education was only for the children who were sufficiently 'recovered' to receive it (Wills 1971, Bridgeland 1971).

However, the Underwood Report also recorded the existence of schools influenced by more traditional thinking about education and care and perhaps influenced by aspects of Approved School provision.

> After an initial period of tolerance, maladjusted children are expected to learn the difference between right and wrong, and that wrong-doing may earn punishment. They can, and should, be treated in many respects just like normal children. (Ministry of Education 1955, p. 76)

Staff in these schools saw maladjusted pupils as being basically normal children, reacting in sometimes extreme or unsociable ways to abnormal childhood experiences. A structured, teacher dominated life-style in an environment which contrasted in size and location but not dramatically in terms of behaviour management from the mainstream might be all that was required.

There is also evidence to suggest that the Ministry of Education (including HMI and the schools medical officers) was never at ease with medical and therapeutic community influence on provision for maladjusted children. In 1960, the Chief Medical Officer wrote that generally:

> children are not capable of making judgements on standards of behaviour, or decisions concerning other children, unless they have reached a level of stability and maturity of judgement at which they can be relied on to do so responsibly. (Ministry of Education 1960, p. 120)

Later, another Senior Medical Officer (DES 1974) stated that, 'Unfortunately after fifty years of child guidance services there is little firm, recorded data about their role and value' (p. 12).

Laslett (1983) rightly noted that Circular 2/75 (DES 1975) which altered assessment procedures and took some power away from school medical officers, marked the growing ascendancy of a more 'educational model'. His earlier book (Laslett 1977) had also reflected the growing recognition of the value of an educational curriculum, although in his view, this was primarily to help the school for the maladjusted to meet its primary purpose of addressing pupils' personal and social development.

Laslett also drew together contemporary views on a number of issues. He recorded that in the view of teachers in the 1970s, the concept of maladjustment covered a wide range of behaviours which included delinquency. He suggested that often the most difficult maladjusted pupils attended London's day rather than residential schools although placement in the latter were used as a means of preventing at risk students from sliding into delinquency, with Child Guidance Clinics referring children to them for social rather than educational reasons. Rates of successful reintegration from maladjusted special schools were low, while a stay of at least two years in a school for the maladjusted was believed necessary for pupils to benefit.

14

Laslett also outlined the limited evidence (to be echoed by Galloway and Goodwin 1979 and Topping 1983) which was available about the efficacy of special schools for the maladjusted. Among the criteria for judging success which he viewed as valid were:

- achieving regular attendance from chronic school refusers;
- preventing children from turning to delinquency;
- leavers obtaining 'even intermittent and transitory employment';
- educational progress as measured in reading tests;
- behavioural progress as measured for example on the Bristol Social Adjustment Scales.

At the same time he made a plea to headteachers and other educators to be more open to audit and to record their achievements for public scrutiny.

The Schools Council Project 1975–1978

The second major enquiry into provision for maladjusted children was conducted by the Schools Council and addressed Laslett's concern for more evidence of good practice. By the time they published their findings (Dawson 1980, Wilson and Evans 1980), much progress had been made on the Underwood recommendations: the national system of psychological services existed and Child Guidance Clinics were retreating into the National Health Service along with some 'medical model' thinking. Many more day schools and special classes attached to mainstream schools existed, although the number of specialist residential schools had also increased (see Table 2.2). Also, building on the model of the London tutorial classes, a variety of special 'units' existed throughout the country.

Table 2.2 Numbers of 'maintained' and non-maintained schools for pupils deemed maladjusted/EBD (Visser and Cole 1996)

1947	1955	1963	1973	1983	Estimate for [1997]
5	33	56	151	220	ca.210

Wilson and Evans (1980) found that most special schools, classes and units now paid only limited attention to the tenets of psychodynamic and therapeutic approaches and despite increasing publicity in the 1970s, of behaviour modification. The majority expressed a strong belief in humanist and cognitive-behaviourist standpoints – what mattered was working through close relationships, attending to needs; reversing a child's expectancy of failure by ensuring regular success in a range of activities which boosted low self-esteem. Counselling (talking to and listening to children) was seen as crucial but could be directive as well as Rogerian. Help targeted on underachievement in basic literacy and numeracy and a general educational approach was seen as important – even as therapy. Maladjusted children were also believed by a clear majority of respondents to need steady routines, structure and discipline. The value of residential schools was also described.

Reference to the Schools Council study will be made again in later chapters as our research design owes much to their model and our findings complement many of theirs.

Lessons from Approved Schools and their CHE successors

There was much to criticise in the punitive, over-regimented regimes of some early approved schools, in which Wills (1967, 1971) participated but later criticised. However, his was a somewhat partisan view as a review published on the back cover of *Spare the Child* recognised. Millham *et al.* (1975) and Hyland (1993) give fairer assessments and some of the better practice recorded by them would seem to have passed down into the schools for children with emotional and behavioural difficulties.

It has already been noted that staff transferred from schools for the maladjusted to approved schools and vice versa, and that it was often a matter of chance whether children went to one sector or to the other. The Dartington Research Unit (Millham *et al.* 1975) provided evidence to support this contention when, with reference to the clientele of approved schools, they commented that 'Much of their crime . . . is casual, unrewarding, ineptly performed and of little more than nuisance value' (p. 17). They also produced a careful, longitudinal study of effective and less effective practice in this sector as it was about to pass into the management of the new social service departments created by the 1969 Children and Young Persons' Act.

Wills (1971) was to praise a revolution at the Cotswold under Richard Balbernie where a traditional approved school was changed into a community espousing therapeutic ideals. Millham *et al.* (1975), however, were distrustful, even disdainful, of what they described as the 'pyschosocial approach', finding more to commend in the more traditional styles of the 'training schools'. They borrowed the language of Bernstein

(1977) to characterise schools as stressing instrumental, expressive and organisational goals to different extents. Their extended participant observation gave rise to their preference for constant-activity, highly organised (by the staff) and purposeful training schools which stressed instrumental goals. They noted that their findings would not be favoured by some social workers and fashionable child care writers but

> boys differ markedly from adults in the sorts of regimes that they enjoy. Some flourish on cross-country runs, maths projects and endless showers, and institutions that provide these should not be viewed as less caring than those which discuss problems at length over cocoa and slices of dripping toast. (Millham *et al.* 1975, p. 84)

Family-group style approved schools were preferred by field social workers. These stressed the affective and pastoral and could be warm and homely but this 'diminished the interest shown in the classroom' (p. 87). Least favoured by Millham *et al.* were two 'therapeutic style' schools described as a 'Pandora's box of acting out adolescents' (p. 92) who did not understand the purpose of the regimes, did not respond to group work and community meetings while unskilled staff became exhausted in attempts 'to control the trivia of institutional life, such as noise levels, bedtimes and meal supervision' (p. 93) and had no energy for deeper pastoral demands. These last two schools were seen to lack purpose, have poorly organised activity programmes and exert little pressure to achieve instrumental goals.

Boys in the Dartington team's sample were found to favour firm, fair, approachable teachers who were skilled in their particular subject. In effective schools the staff were clearly in control and impinged on the boys' world, fragmenting incipient delinquent subcultures and having lasting beneficial effects on children's behaviour. In these schools, staff were said to relentlessly hammer home orthodox attitudes and aspirations which paid off in leavers who were more resistant to criminal tendencies than pupils in schools where intensive individual counselling and casework had been offered. They also noted that schools which stressed pastoral care tended to achieve better results and that the quality of pastoral care was related to the extent of the commitment of the staff to the school's goals. Pupils also appreciated the efforts of staff in providing high quality vocational and trade training, which often resulted in a high percentage of leavers finding employment (see also Hyland 1993).

After 1969, attempts were made to foster a more child-centred approach notably through *Care and Treatment in a Planned Environment* (DHSS 1970), a publication which says much that is relevant to work with pupils with EBD. A humanist approach, which pervades much good child care writing (e.g. Ainsworth and Fulcher 1981) is stressed while Maslow's (1943, 1970) hierarchy of needs underpins the emphasis placed on meeting physical needs, giving a sense of security, building self-esteem through achievement and helping a healthy dependence grow into independence. 'Milieu therapy' and the creative use of 'life-space' are also acknowledged: all aspects of the child's day should be used to foster emotional and social growth. However, possibly reflecting 'social services' as opposed to educational or Home Office thinking, routines and rules have a place but organised systems of rewards and sanctions do not: instead trust is placed in the power of staff–pupil relationships. There must be allowance for privacy – for example, through the 'individualised bed space' and for other aspects of child care practice which respect the dignity of the child (echoed in Maier 1981) and positive group work.

In the event the high hopes of this document were not realised in practice. The blueprint led to increased staff costs while rates of reoffending among leavers, low in the 1930s, 1940s and 1950s rose to very high levels. Within twenty years most of the CHEs had closed (Hyland 1993). It is likely that some of the candidates who were previously placed in CHEs now came into a burgeoning provision for the maladjusted which in turn provided new careers for some of their erstwhile teachers and care workers.

Developments in the 1980s and 1990s

There were clear lessons to be learnt by schools for children with emotional and behavioural difficulties from the Approved Schools, notably how to provide education. In the 1980s, HMI (DES 1978c) castigated narrow curriculum and low standards there as well as in special schools (DES 1989b) and the arrival of the National Curriculum must have been welcomed by the inspectorate. If students were not formally disapplied from sections of the National Curriculum, as was usually the case, schools had to comply with its requirements. This has had a dramatic effect on some schools as Grimshaw with Berridge (1994) and our own survey indicate. While psychotherapists such as Orr (1995) and some teachers (e.g. Marchant 1995) condemned it, early evidence suggested that many headteachers found the general idea if not all the realities of implementation to their liking (Davies and Landman 1991, Lund 1992). Our research aimed to check out these impressions and also reactions to other major changes such as local management of schools and its consequences for the relationship between the LEA and the special school.

We also wished to see the extent of the influence of The Elton Report (DES 1989a), with its advocacy of whole-school preventative approaches to behaviour management and the need for all teachers to learn and apply basic classroom techniques and to display more 'withitness' (Kounin 1977). These messages fed into Circular 8/94 (DfE 1994a) *Pupil Behaviour and Discipline*, and have been carried forward in the current advice on the education of children with EBD (Circular 9/94, DfE 1994b).

A question which particularly concerned us was whether HMI are right in seeing no essential differences between effective teaching of mainstream children in 'ordinary schools' and pupils with EBD in special schools. Indeed, are HMI right to extrapolate so many of the lessons from the literature on school effectiveness from the 1980s and early 1990s to the special schools? As a preliminary stage in our project we studied key 'effectiveness' and 'school improvement' texts including those of Rutter *et al.* (1979), Mortimore *et al.* (1983), Galloway (1990), Ainscow (1991), Reynolds and Cuttance (1992) and Stoll and Fink (1994). Having done so, we agree with Cooper *et al.*'s (1994) verdict that they do have relevance and we reproduce Charlton and David's (1993) 11 key 'effectiveness' factors as ones which we also felt characterise schools which successfully manage difficult behaviour:

1. effective, consultative style of leadership of headteacher and SMT which takes into account pupil and parent opinion;
2. clear school-wide policies on education and behaviour management which are meaningful to pupils and consistently and humanely enforced;
3. differentiated curricula;
4. high but not unreasonable academic expectations;
5. positive attitude to pupil behaviour with more rewards than sanctions;
6. high professional standards (efficient planning, setting, marking, punctuality);
7. skilful teaching which arouses pupil interest and motivates;
8. preventative rather than reactive strategies to classroom disruption;
9. supportive and respectful relationships between all adults and pupils in the school system;
10. involvement of pupils in school's life; giving pupils responsibility;
11. an effective system of pastoral care.

These and other ideas from the school improvement literature influenced us as we set about our project. We also considered two studies

(Cooper 1993, Grimshaw with Berridge 1994) which looked at residential schools for pupils with EBD. Cooper's account of residential schooling found pupils being helped in three major areas – respite, relationships and resignification. Children from complicated and sometimes fraught family backgrounds and unsatisfactory mainstream experiences were seen to be provided with respite in boarding schools where they were able to form beneficial relationships with staff and peers. They were provided with learning experiences and emotional support which enabled them to cast off the negative labels with which they had been tagged and according to which they had lived, resignifying themselves in a new positive light. Would we find echoes of Cooper's 3Rs in our research? Cooper also suggested that mainstream schools seeking to improve effectiveness could usefully follow some special school practice.

Grimshaw with Berridge conducted a detailed study of four contrasting boarding schools looking at the circumstances and progress of 67 children and their families. Why was it that these schools could apparently achieve what the less restrictive environments failed to deliver? There was not orderly progression from least restrictive mainstream placement to most restrictive residential school as Topping (1983) would have wished. Students arrived in residential provision in haphazard manner when the resources of mainstream schools, support services and families were exhausted, usually caused by the child's challenging behaviour. Referrals were socially not educationally driven. Many parents bemoaned that more could and should have been done to make residential placement unnecessary but once it had happened 73 per cent did not wish their child to leave the boarding school. Better family relationships and increased contact were reported by many. Some educational and behavioural progress was noted but was usually achieved by 'ordinary' methods both in class and in the care situation. Topping's (1983) notion of 'spontaneous remission' is questioned as the treatment received in the boarding school is likely to be little different to the treatment which might be given in less restrictive environments, involving 'a range of rather ordinary measures of guidance and support' (p. 133).

There are interesting parallels with Millham *et al.* (1975). School 2, in Grimshaw with Berridge's sample, exemplifying the 'personalised group care model' with an emphasis on individual therapeutic intervention, has more difficulty in controlling behaviour than a highly structured, behaviourist leaning school which achieves high academic results and where 'mild words were sufficient to exercise control'. Here the pupils have to sit up in silence at the end of meals and sometimes stand in lines, but the authors comment that:

> Despite the formal ethos of the school there was a relationship between teachers and pupils that at times included expressions of warmth and humour. (p. 79)

Did the all-pervasive points system indicate the school's acceptance of the ideas of behaviourists such as Skinner and Watson or were they imported by refugee staff from CHEs?

Finally, Grimshaw with Berridge were much concerned with abuse. They reported that 21 per cent of the children were said to have 'experienced some form of suspected or confirmed abuse' in the last year. They then write, 'Data was (sic) not gathered from staff about who was responsible or where the abuse had taken place'. Did they mean to make the jump from 'suspected abuse' to the apparent assertion that it actually occurred? It would also have been helpful if more detail had been given (as discussed in Chapter 5). In the light of the various abuse cases which have beset the field of child care and education in the last decade, continuing vigilance is clearly required.

This leads to the 1989 Children Act and its impact on work with children with EBD. Has it been a help or a hindrance; a necessary safeguard or actually harmful to the very children it was designed to protect? Its concern for children's rights and the involvement of the young person in decisions relating to his or her schooling and care echoes the effective schools' advice that pupils should have a voice and that schools should seek it out and listen to it. This will not be a new message to espousers of the psychodynamic or humanist approach or 1990s believers in cognitive-behaviourism. It seemed likely as we started our project that EBD schools would find the idea of children's rights easy to live with in most respects. The one exception we expected was in relation to physical restraint. Was the absence of clear guidance from the Department of Health and from DfEE as important as our informal contacts suggested? How did schools cope? Did they differ in their approaches, one from another or in comparison with practice in children's homes? These appeared very live issues in the early 1990s which our supplementary questionnaire on the Children Act and physical restraint in particular set out to probe (see Appendix 1).

Government guidance in the mid-1990s

At the time of writing another 'catch-all' definition of mal-adjustment/EBD exists in government guidance (Circular 9/94):

> Children with EBD are on a continuum. Their problems are clearer and greater than sporadic naughtiness or moodiness and yet not so great as to be classed as mental illness. (DfE 1994b, p. 4)

They range from 'social maladaption to abnormal emotional stresses' (p. 7); 'are persistent and constitute learning difficulties' (p. 7). There follows detailed amplification in which within-child emotional factors are counterpoised with difficult externalised behaviour including truancy, aggression, violence and destructive behaviour. Children with EBD are seen as having problems in relationships but causes are described as complex and involving school and home factors. Determining whether a child has EBD depends on 'frequency, persistence, severity or abnormality and cumulative effect of the behaviour in context compared to other children' (p. 8). A section at the end of the circular is devoted to children at the psychiatric end of the spectrum for whom meaningful inter-agency working, with substantial input from specialist services, is seen as essential; children who in the past, like a number of other groups referred to in the circular, did not necessarily fall within the educational net.

At the same time the advice given takes into account many of the ideas discussed earlier in this chapter. It recognises that EBD arise from a mixture of factors 'within' and 'outwith' the child and notes the possibility of 'spontaneous remission'; that early identification can aid speedy 'recovery'; the importance of school ethos in the mainstream which can reduce the need for segregation; the need for partnership with parents and for pupil involvement in setting and organising learning goals and monitoring progress. It takes into account the staged assessment procedures introduced by the Code of Practice (DfE, 1994d).

The fourth section of Circular 9/94 is devoted to special schools. Children in these can present 'a considerable challenge' (p. 23) but the circular acknowledges that with appropriate organisation, careful curricular planning and good teaching and care, their needs can be met. Significantly, it states:

> All of the general points made in this Circular in relation to mainstream education about developing a school ethos capable of allowing children with emotional and behaviour difficulties to develop; the need to ensure access to the curriculum; the overriding need to develop children's self-esteem; and positive reinforcement apply also to special schools. (p. 23)

The circular clearly advocates carrying forward 'normal' and 'mainstream' type approaches into special schools but recognises that extra time is needed to assist residential pupils to 'catch up' in basic skills. It notes that the National Curriculum must be delivered and suggests that small schools hire part-time and peripatetic specialists to cover areas in which full-time staffing is deficient. Staff are advised to 'establish firm boundaries of behaviour for all pupils. Good standards of behaviour should be the norm' (p. 24) before advice, which applies equally to mainstream schools, is given on the creation of positive, whole-school behaviour policies.

However, it is recognised that emphasis on the affective and expressive needs of children to assist their personal and social development is essential; that staff should look at the emotions beneath the surface behaviour and be aware of the theoretical perspectives to which reference has been made above. Education (in the form of remedial help in literacy skills) is seen as building pupils' morale and self-esteem and there are references to the importance of children's psychological needs: school systems must offer security, the opportunity to initiate and maintain good relationships with adults and peers and encourage personal growth towards maturity. There is also awareness that teaching style has to be carefully attuned to pupils' learning styles as adherents of behaviourist, cognitive–behaviourist theory and ecosystemic approaches advise (see Ayers *et al.* 1995, Cooper *et al.* 1994). Thus we are advised that 'it is important to set short-term targets and goals which will stretch but not overwhelm them, to involve them in the formation of these learning goals and to establish high expectations of their performance' (p. 23). The implication is that a collaborative approach to learning can help pupils to break out of negative cycles of pessimistic thinking in which they may be locked.

The section on residential schooling raises worries about costs but recognises that boarding can be beneficial where learning difficulties exist and/or 'where family support is lacking or inadequate, or family influence is damaging' (p. 27). Reference is later made to some pupils' emotional needs requiring 'a consistent environment, providing a different lifestyle in a structured and predictable regime effectively for 24 hours a day, for the child to benefit from a suitable educational curriculum' (p. 28). It is stressed that where placement is essentially socially driven, then social services should bear at least some of the costs.

Comment on the 'green paper' on special education (DfEE 1997) is not made here as it had not been published when we conducted our research and consequently did not influence it.

Conclusion

In this chapter we have sketched salient research findings, ideas and dilemmas from the past as well as key points from recent official publications which prompted the questions we asked in our survey and programme of visits to schools. Limitations on space precluded detailed description on individual theoretical perspectives. These are covered in Wilson and Evans (1980), Whittaker (1981), Apter (1982), Upton (1992), Cooper *et al.* (1994), Ayers *et al.* (1995) and Garner and Gains (1996). Like many practitioners, we see value in aspects of biophysical, psychodynamic, humanist, cognitive–behaviourist, behaviourist and sociological explanations for children's emotional and behavioural difficulties. We recognise the conjunction of both external and internal forces producing a child's behaviour and see the various perspectives coming together in the ecosystemic view outlined by Cooper *et al.* (1994). It is essential for staff to understand the varied aetiology of behaviour and to appreciate the complicated interactions between different aspects of a child's ecosystem if proficient and individualised education and care programming is to be offered.

Chapter 3

Pupils and Parents: Who Are They?

For effectiveness in provision for children with EBD it would seem essential that the characteristics of the client group – both pupils and parents – are clearly understood in order to provide a secure base for appropriate responses at both institutional and individual level. This may seem an obvious comment, but the history of special provision suggests that it is highly significant (Aichhorn 1951, Millham *et al.* 1975). In too many institutions neither the pupils nor their families appear to have been at the centre of staff thinking; instead, organisational goals relating to survival of the institution or to making life easier for the staff seem to have predominated. In this chapter, in order to emphasise the centrality of the child and his or her family, we outline the characteristics of the pupils attending EBD schools and of their families before, in later chapters, describing the staff and the provision made in the schools.

The survey sample

Returns to our survey suggest that there were close to 7,000 children attending the 156 sample schools. We judge it safer to give an approximate figure because the numbers attending EBD schools can fluctuate from week to week as transfers in, and out, are sometimes made in haphazard fashion when dormant crises erupt (Grimshaw with Berridge 1994) or, suddenly for therapeutic communities at least, funding becomes available (Clough 1997). Also, our questionnaire was answered over a period of some months and some entries might have been estimated averages made from memory.

Predictably there were far fewer children in the schools at primary level than at secondary. Despite increasing exclusions from primary schools (Hayden 1997) far more pupils receive behavioural 'statements' and enter special schools in the early and mid-stages of the secondary phase. Our data also indicate that only a minority of children who attend EBD schools at primary stage re-enter mainstream secondary education. Of our sample, under 3 per cent or less than 200 children were at Key Stage 1 (KS1), rising to 25 per cent at Key Stage 2 (KS2) and peaking at 39 per cent at Key Stage 3 (KS3). At Key Stage 4 (KS4) the number falls back to 31 per cent and 2 per cent are young people who have 'stayed on'. The major reason for the apparent decline in numbers of senior pupils is that KS4 consists of only two year groups. However, our visits to schools suggest that some older pupils are voting with their feet, unattracted by what the schools offer, while others are being excluded . These young people will tend to be enrolled at Pupil Referral Units (PRUs) or perhaps join the ranks of the 'lost children' who receive home tuition or sometimes no education at all. One of the schools visited claimed that about 30 per cent of the pupils admitted did not 'last the course'.

About 40 per cent (over 2,500) of the sample boarded for some, or less frequently for all, of the week. Data from our interviews show that some schools use day attendance as a first step towards residential placement. If the family has reservations about boarding this can help to establish relationships before boarding is tried. Conversely, towards the end of a child's career, full-time boarders increasingly become day pupils as preparation for leaving and independence. The confidence with which staff operate these flexible approaches suggests that the fears of some schools about 'contamination' of settled boarders by day pupils may be exaggerated.

Visser and Cole (1996) reported that boys in schools for EBD pupils outnumbered girls by about 12 to 1. The schools responding to our questionnaire had an overall ratio of 10:1, although the gap narrowed to 8:1 at KS4. All these ratios show a marked increase on the 5:1 ratio found by Dawson (1980). Some schools registered with DfEE as mixed schools have ceased to admit girls but in mixed-gender schools generally boys heavily outnumber girls: the most striking example was one girl to 72 boys in one school, while it was common to find four or five girls to 30, 40 or 50 boys. Ratios in approved independent schools (AIs) are generally more favourable (their catchment areas often include many Local Education Authorities (LEAs) and Social Services Departments (SSDs)) and in two such schools the girls narrowly outnumbered the boys. We discovered four schools in England for girls only: two were small 'registered' independent schools and two were LEA schools. Some 40 per cent of the sample schools were for boys only.

Staff attitudes towards admitting female pupils vary. Our interview data suggest strong feelings in some all-boys schools that it would be inadvisable for them to become mixed. Staff used only to working with boys are nervous about being able to cope with girls and the latter are seen as a threat to the established positive ethos of the schools. Conversely, in some schools which, through lack of referrals of girls, have been forced to become single-sex, there is regret. They tend to share the views expressed by colleagues in mixed schools that it is more 'natural' to mix the sexes and that it aids social skills development while nonetheless arguing that the management of girls with EBD can be more demanding than that of boys. Also, mixed-schools were seen to present practical management problems and staffing problems; arranging for female staff to be on duty in school when an individual girl needs to be taken off site, for a medical for example, can pose a problem.

The questionnaire survey did not explore the issue of race. However, the evidence from the OFSTED reports and the observations we made on our visits suggests that the conclusions drawn by Cooper *et al.* (1991a) may need revisiting. Osler (1997) points to the continuing disproportionate number of black pupils who are excluded from mainstream schools but black pupils are not over-represented in many schools for pupils with EBD. Typically, in schools at some distance from major conurbations, there are no, or very few, pupils from ethnic minority groups or of mixed-race. However, in a school close to Birmingham, for example, there were close to 20 per cent, and in a school, whose clientele came mainly from London, over a third. In a northern inner city LEA with four EBD schools we were told that the majority of black pupils opted to attend one of these schools in preference to the other three schools for pupils with EBD although this is obviously a statement which is open to challenge and interpretation. While we have no data for our sample, overall a picture emerges which suggests that the representation of minority ethnic groups in EBD schools across the country is uneven and may have changed in recent years; a finding which suggests the need for further and more detailed research.

The nature of emotional and behavioural difficulties

Wilson and Evans (1980) reported that children displaying acting out, delinquent or disruptive behaviour were far more likely to attend special provision than pupils with emotional disturbance. Was this still the case? Recent concerns about the 'emotional' component of the term EBD being lost (Bowers 1996) added to our wish to explore this issue. Sadly, the precision of the respondents' answers varied and half either found it difficult or impossible to separate behavioural from emotional difficulties; they were seen to be inextricably linked. However, our data do make clear that a special school placement is still far more commonly triggered by overt and disruptive behaviour than by the identification of emotional difficulties. This is consistent with Grimshaw with Berridge's (1994) analysis of entries to four contrasting residential schools for children with EBD and we were left agreeing with Galloway and Goodwin (1987) that referrals to special schools commonly involves children whose behaviour had disturbed mainstream schools beyond their levels of tolerance. It was not that the identified behaviour constituted learning difficulties for the pupils deemed EBD, although it usually did: it was more that the behaviour was seen to cause learning difficulties for their mainstream peers.

However, this was not the full picture. Certainly, the special schools are aware of the emotional underpinnings of much their pupils' behaviour and some schools, echoing Vivian (1994), claimed that their recent intakes included increasing numbers of boys with internalised difficulties. This was seen in questionnaire data from some schools in the independent sector, who can perhaps be more choosy about whom they admit. Some of our interviewees on the school visits also stressed that the emotional difficulties were increasing – although usually in tandem with difficult externalised behaviour. One headteacher talked of 'baby-sitting' four pupils who previously would have attended a therapeutic community.

The quotations below, taken from our data, support the use of the wide definition of EBD given in Circular 9/94 (DfE 1994b), from fringe-delinquency/social maladaption to pronounced emotional and even psychiatric problems. However, it was clear that many schools felt very strongly that the severity of their pupils' difficulties was increasing. When asked if the nature of their intake had changed in the last five years, 83 per cent answered in the affirmative. The adjective 'more' appeared in respondents' and interviewees' answers with persistent regularity:

Criminality and violence

'More delinquent pupils, little respect for authority of parents. Trouble with police.' [M005]

'We get a majority of Year 5 and 6 pupils and almost all are hostile/aggressive. No other category of EBD is referred.' [M014]

'Less emotional problems, more aggressive and violent behaviour.' [M016]

'Pupils are far more aggressive – as are their parents.' [M031]

'More violent and aggressive. More likely to attack staff and other pupils.' [M069]

'A large proportion of recent referrals have had violent, criminal or other major conduct disorders.' [M162]

'— shire now has an inclusive policy. The pupil intake is now more difficult, challenging and violent.' [M178]

Increasing family and social problems

'More social deprivation.' [M001]

'Far more complex needs related to disfunctioning families and communities in the area.' [M087]

'Greater Social Service part funding with subsequent increase in percentage of delinquent boys and reduced family support.' [A14]

'More abused children.' [M137]

Learning difficulties

'Children's ability plummeted.' [M137]

Psychiatric difficulties

'Some children who as adolescents or as adults might be assessed under mental health regulations and "sectioned" are our responsibility "to hold" – there doesn't seem to be any provision available to manage them.' [M030]

Age

'More extreme behavioural difficulties – younger and younger.' [M189]

(On new Year 7 intake): 'Extraordinary levels of defiance and aggression.' [M129]

Finally, we give a quotation which summarises the feelings of many respondents and staff interviewed on our visits:

'Greater complexity of EBD – behaviour and emotions now at extremes . . .' [M108]

The returns to the survey (confirmed in our visits) also indicated that some schools contained children on the autistic spectrum; often diagnosed as having Asberger's Syndrome or occasionally Tourettes and other rare conditions. One headteacher who we interviewed reported specific learning difficulties, epilepsy and diabetes following the closure of a residential school in his county which had previously catered for these children.

Attention deficit/hyperactivity disorder was also mentioned in questionnaire returns as a reason for referral to schools but only for a small minority of children. In contrast, when the acting headteacher of an inner-city school, in the presence of the authors, asked a class of ten pupils how many children were on 'Ritalin', five hands were raised.

Interviews also alluded to the problems of students returning from weekends and holidays either with drugs or alcohol in their possession or shaking off the 'hangovers' of 'indulging' while at home. A strong feeling existed that for some young people substance abuse was leading to a degree of volatility and moodiness far greater than that which existed a decade ago.

Is EBD differentiated from delinquency?

With the closure of many residential establishments designed for young offenders and many other social services residential facilities, it might have been supposed that EBD schools would be receiving many more children with criminal records or, at least, police involvement. As suggested by some of the statements reported above, this is a problem for certain schools and discussions with owners of some independent schools suggest that they see their future 'market' as 'looking after' fourteen-year-olds with confirmed delinquent tendencies. However, confirming the research of Beedell (1993) and Grimshaw (1995), for the majority of our sample delinquency is not a seen as a major criterion for referral.

It can be seen in Table 3.1 that 40 per cent of the respondents indicated that under 10 per cent of their present pupils had been cautioned or charged by police before admission to the EBD school. Three of the four schools who said that 70 per cent or more of admissions had been cautioned or charged were small independent schools apparently catering for 'looked after' children. Over 26 per cent of the replies suggested that the number of pupils being cautioned or charged lessens after admission while about 9 per cent suggested that it increases. This accords with the view that special schools and, in particular, residential placement can help reduce juvenile crime (Ministry of Education 1946); a view which some interviewees in the good practice schools agreed with. However, they did not necessarily put this down to their success in radically altering children's criminal propensities but (echoing McGavin 1997) rather to the more prosaic fact that the pupils were now gainfully occupied in school rather than footloose truants or permanently excluded youngsters receiving minimal home tuition and spending the bulk of their time on the streets looking for excitement. This is a potentially important function of special schooling which should enter 'value for money' analyses and is worthy of more detailed research.

Table 3.1 Pupils cautioned or charged by the police before/since admission

	under 10% of pupils	10–25%	26–50%	51–70%	over 70%
Before admission	40	31	21	5	3
Since admission	51	32	12	1.5	3.5

Table 3.1 also suggests that children deemed EBD, like their Victorian and early-twentieth century forerunners, continue to straddle the divide between special educational needs and delinquency that requires court decisions and prolonged Home Office or social services involvement. Later it is shown that headteachers in our sample, as their predecessors, prefer to cater for students whose delinquency is of a low order and who can be diverted early from delinquent careers. However, schools are sometimes forced to admit pupils who have committed burglaries, assault, car theft and even arson and attempted rape. Senior staff see themselves as successful if they manage to hold on to these pupils without further offences being committed whilst the pupils are in school.

The parameters of provision

It has long been held (see Ministry of Education 1955), although without much evidence, that a clear admissions policy is a necessary requirement for effective practice. Similar views continue to be expressed with calls for the EBD category to be broken down into discrete parts (Cooper 1996); dividing, for example, vulnerable children where the 'E' predominates from more aggressive and 'street-wise' pupils who might make life unpleasant for the former. Having pupils whom staff are convinced are wrongly placed and/or who are seriously upsetting the fragile ecosystem of a school seems inimical to effectiveness yet pre-admission interviews and written reports on a child can be misleading. It was certainly the experience of one of the writers that unwarranted images of two-headed monsters are sometimes conjured up in these reports in relation to pupils who settle, cause few problems and thrive. Conversely, it was not uncommon for information describing a child's most challenging behaviour or criminal activities to be withheld by agencies desperate to persuade the school to admit a pupil. In the interests of the other pupils and of the child itself, it is obviously incumbent on the admitting school to try to obtain as accurate a picture of the child as possible. Equally, judgements have to be made on the skills and motives of those who write reports and a good deal of intuition is needed when the child and his family are interviewed.

In the event, headteachers of LEA schools in our survey often do not have a choice, having to accept whoever is referred to them. Away from large authorities, where a choice of EBD schools exist within comfortable daily travelling distance from the pupils' homes, the LEA practice of using its own facilities, sometimes comprising only one or two schools, has taken precedence over seeking out of borough or out of county placements which the professionals might perceive as better meeting a child's needs (the pupil may think differently). Shortage of places and cold financial realities, or sometimes parental and pupil preference, have made selecting pupils a difficult business with headteachers having to make the best of an imperfect situation. Our survey shows that this continued in 1996/7.

However, the questionnaire does show that schools do resist strongly admitting students with a record of violent behaviour which might cause bodily harm to other pupils and staff. In response to a question asking the respondents to name up to three types of behaviour which would prompt the headteacher to oppose admission of potential pupils, around 40 per cent suggested violence and 20 per cent delinquency, while children with histories of substance abuse and fire-raising were also viewed with much circumspection (see Table 3.2).

Table 3.2 Most common reasons for opposing the admission of potential pupils (number of nominations)

1. Violence (general [54]; to staff [8])	62
2. Delinquency	32
3. Sexual abuse/problems	30
4. Psychiatric problems	26
5. Drugs	21
6. Arson	19
7. SSD/'looked after children'	14
8. Low ability/learning difficulties	12
9. Age (usually Year 10 or 11)	11
10. No parental support	10

Predictably, worries about sexual behaviour, always a concern, but perhaps more so since the 1989 Children Act and recent abuse scandals, figure prominently. And while official definitions of emotional and behavioural difficulties have always seen pupils with severe psychiatric disorders as being at one end of the EBD spectrum, it can be seen in Table 3.2 that there are serious concerns about admitting these pupils too.

Similarly, it can be seen that worry was expressed about the admission of children 'looked after' by local social services departments. In its official literature, one survey school stated that the purposes of residence were to ensure attendance and 'a stable level of care provision and continuity of experience outside school hours'. However,

> The LEA does not provide boarding places in purely social circumstances such as parental request, stress at home, single parenthood or where a child is 'at risk'. In these circumstances Social Services may become involved in decision making. [M150]

According to the literature, this statement of intent is not mirrored by practice in many schools. Gemal's (1993) study of the children attending one LEA's residential school found that about 75 per cent of the pupils had social services involvement, 100 per cent presented problems (usually verbal and physical aggression) at home and 30 per cent in their neighbourhood. A recent Social Services Inspectorate/OFSTED study (1995) of four local authorities found that 9.6 per cent of the 'looked after' children had statements for EBD and many of these attended special schools. Many social services departments appear ready to pay for pupils to attend independent residential schools and take advantage of holiday care possibly because chronic problems persist in finding suitable alternatives such as foster homes where these children will actually settle (Aldgate *et al*. 1989) or children's homes staffed by social workers who are sufficiently skilled in managing challenging behaviour (Chaplain and Freeman 1994).

The results of the present study confirm that EBD schools continue, as they always have done (see Weaver 1968, McNair 1968, Cole 1986, Grimshaw with Berridge 1994), to have a pronounced social work function. The headteacher of a day school noted that his school was a 'single agency doing multi-agency work'; in the past this has applied with greater force to residential schools. The latter are often the only anchor some children have in their turbulent lives, providing them with a home of sorts for up to fifty-two weeks of the year. These children were described by a headteacher whom we interviewed as 'nomads', while Reid (cited in Moss 1968) used the term 'orphans of the living' (p. 28). Not surprisingly, it was a common statement in questionnaire and interview answers that the most 'difficult' children were the rootless 'looked after' children.

In Table 3.2 the need to have at least the acquiescence of the child's family is also noted as an important consideration at admission. If there is active opposition from the parents then some headteachers believe that the chances of 'winning through' with the student are severely hampered. We discuss this, and 'ability levels' and age of admission in more detail below.

Respondents were also asked to nominate three reasons which would prompt headteachers to permanently exclude pupils. A similar picture to that summarised in Table 3.2 emerged. Serious violence, whether to fellow pupils or to staff, was most frequently nominated, with 'beyond school discipline/repeated severe disruption' in second place. Drug abuse, arson, delinquency and sexual abuse were also commonly mentioned. To these were added 'damage to school property'.

The cognitive functioning of pupils with EBD

Any judgement on the effectiveness of a school for pupils with EBD must take into account the children's cognitive functioning and levels of achievement in core subjects on entry to the school. To do this a baseline needs to be established, including an assessment of innate and environmental factors impinging on a child's performance in class, to enable 'value added' assessments of the school's achievement. The Schools Council Survey (Dawson 1980) recognised the importance of 'baselining'. Their study collected data on IQs. We repeated this exercise using a question relating to 'learning difficulties' rather than the now outmoded notion of general intelligence. The results summarised in Table

3.3 are similar to those of Dawson's study with 19 per cent having 'below average' IQs, 43 per cent 'average (low)', 29 per cent 'average (high)' and only 9 per cent 'above average'.

Table 3.3 Ability levels of pupils in schools for pupils with EBD

Significant Learning Difficulties not caused by EBD	c.18%
Mild Learning Difficulties not caused by EBD	c.25%
Of average ability	c.47%
Above average ability	c.10%

The Schools Council Project also found that most entrants to schools for the maladjusted (as they were then called) had fallen behind in basic subjects. Again Dawson's findings were mirrored by our own. In our survey, about 50 per cent of pupils were reported to be 'significant underachievers' in the core areas of English, Maths and Science. In addition, around 30 per cent were said to be 'serious underachievers' in the three subjects. We are aware that these are 'broad brush' indicators but they do suggest that pupils come to EBD special schools with much ground to make up if they are to have any chance of passing nationally accredited examinations – particularly if they are not entering the special school until Years 8, 9, 10 and very occasionally Year 11.

Enabling pupils to make progress in the curriculum is a challenge for teachers, particularly when the pupils' attitude to work and their classroom behaviour impact negatively on their own learning and create learning difficulties for their classmates. These are the main reasons why pupils are referred to EBD special schools and these difficulties do not immediately disappear upon arrival in the special school, whatever the skills of the staff. This is clear from the answers of respondents when asked to comment on the learning style of their pupils. In their answers references were frequently made to short attention span, low self-esteem, fear of new material which might lead to more failure, mercurial temperament, distractibility, reluctance and difficulties in putting pen to paper or exploring their feelings. These character traits are revisited when teaching content and approaches are discussed in Chapter 6.

Dawson found that only two per cent of the Schools Council sample had IQs 'very much above average'. This finding is also mirrored by our own; only a small minority of pupils were rated as being of above average ability. This suggests that 'gifted' pupils are less often identified by mainstream schools as having EBD; typically, the EBD pupil will have mild or significant learning difficulties and will be underachieving in core subjects. These learning difficulties are likely to be exacerbated by their behavioural difficulties.

Natural and corporate parenting

In many cases children's difficulties are further compounded by their family situations; indeed the problems may have been created by the latter. On one visit the headteacher of the school expressed the view that 90 per cent of the children's difficulties could be attributed to their home circumstances. On another visit we were told that only 15 per cent of the children on the roll of a day EBD school lived in a traditional setting with two birth-parents. In this section some of the difficulties encountered in the home and the nature of the family backgrounds of pupils attending EBD special schools are sketched.

The importance of family background has been a focus of previous research. Cooper (1993), for example, after extended study of pupils attending two residential schools concluded that not only did the schools offer escape from difficult and stressful day schools, but also from fraught family situations. Earlier reference to this function of residential provision is to be found in Laslett (1977) while Grimshaw with Berridge (1994) added to our knowledge of the family's contribution to EBD when they obtained data from a sample of 41 parents of pupils attending four residential special schools. Of these, 63 per cent referred to the difficulties they had in controlling the behaviour of the children at home (see also Gemal 1993); 18 per cent mentioned problems between the child attending residential school and his or her siblings; 16 per cent talked of stealing; and 15 per cent of destructiveness.

It is possible to paint a stereotypical picture of the pupil with EBD where social deprivation, dysfunctional family life and poverty are the norm. For many this will be accurate but it is not a complete picture. Pupils with EBD can come from a wide range of backgrounds including well-to-do middle class families although there is a tendency for these children's difficulties to be more often described in terms of biological or genetic conditions, i.e. those who are coming to be described as the 'syndromic children' (Asberger's, Tourette's and ADHD).

Interviewees in the present study commonly alluded to loving but somewhat skewed parenting. An overly punitive approach could be mingled with the giving of expensive gifts; families might have adopted a 'laissez-faire' approach, either because this had always been their way or because they had fought unsuccessfully to control difficult behaviour and now found it easier to give in to a child's requests however unreasonable.

A day school headteacher talked of parents being firm but not fair: he mentioned parents who frequently locked their child in his room for extended periods. Their heart was in the right place but their approach to managing the child's behaviour could be over-punitive or constant nagging which made a chronically difficult situation worse.

Certain themes emerge in our data about the family backgrounds which confirm past findings:

- broken marriages are very common;
- lone parents struggle to cope financially;
- problems are encountered with the pupil's siblings, e.g. delinquency, learning difficulties or health problems;
- relationship problems between child with EBD and mother's new partner or with step-siblings;
- unsuitable role models for child, e.g. parent involved in drugs or recidivist;
- psychiatric difficulties, e.g. mother depressive and has attempted suicide;
- physical abuse in some households.

In contrast to the articulate nature and successful education of some, many parents were reported to have had educational difficulties of their own which have left them with bitter memories from their school days. This in turn colours their perception of their children's schooling and teachers and suspicion and hatred may stand in the way of building positive relationships. This may explain the aggression and hostility which was reported in our survey as often being exhibited towards staff. The deputy headteacher of one school summarised the attitude of many parents whom he claimed would say, 'Don't send my son home with homework as I can't read myself'. A headteacher of a day school commented on the low educational self-image of many of his pupils' parents, whose attitude he reported as: 'I was no good at school. He's the same.' This headteacher doubted if helping children to the correct levels of attainment in the full range of National Curriculum subjects held much importance for these parents. Conversely, we heard of parents whose over-expectations for their offspring and inability to hide their disappointment at their child's lack of progress could lead to worsening relationships between parent and child and possibly to the creation of 'secondary deviance' or EBD.

Many pupils with EBD in special schools have no regular family base. On one school visit we were told by the deputy headteacher that 90 per cent of those attending the school returned to their family home for holidays while 10 per cent were 'looked after' by the local social services. At a day school, about 25 per cent of the school role consisted of 'looked after' children. At another school which did not form part of the final study, up to a third of the children on roll had social work involvement and sometimes 20 per cent of the population from perhaps a dozen different local authorities would remain at school for most of the school holidays because of the lack of suitable alternatives in their home areas. These children were described to the authors as 'nomads'. Contact with their families was either forbidden or fleeting. These youngsters need carefully planned 'corporate parenting' with agencies working together on behalf of the child (SSI/OFSTED 1995, DfE 1994c) to ensure that a child has a regular place either with the same foster parents or at a children's home for weekends or holidays. Echoing Laslett (1977), our survey and interviews indicate that many 'social services' children should not be placed long-term in schools for children with EBD. They are doubly disadvantaged, and yet if better alternatives do not exist, what else can be offered?

The need for pupils to have consistent parenting applies to those in day as well as residential schools. Senior staff's views on the frequently poor quality service provided by some overstretched and under-resourced social services departments in relation to their pupils is discussed later. However, references made in various interviews to the lack of ability of children's home staff to control and motivate youngsters with EBD does need noting here. In line with the findings of SSI/OFSTED (1995) 'home' experiences and perceptions are seen as impacting negatively on the children's performance and behaviour in school.

Conclusion

A senior teacher in a residential school remarked to one of the authors:

> 'What is EBD? Basically what someone else has put down on paper. We then have to take their label off and look underneath?' [M158]

In the pages above we too have tried to 'peel back' a confusing and imprecise label, an essential task for those who are serious about responding effectively to meeting the needs of pupils with EBD. Staff have to view the verdicts of the professionals from a pupil's previous life with much scepticism if the child is to be enabled to make a fresh start in the special school. Teachers, case workers and others also have to work hard to empathise and build relationships with the child's often alienated and suspicious carers. In the next chapter we look at the characteristics of the people who endeavour to achieve this.

Chapter 4

The Characteristics of Staff Working in Schools for Pupils with EBD

'It is profoundly true,' wrote Wilson and Evans (1980), 'that the quality of any provision for children will depend on the quality of the people who run it' (p. 80). Similarly, Franklin (1945), stated that she did 'not think that it can be too much emphasised that in planned environmental therapy the staff are the most important factor' (p. 14). These are sentiments we endorse. The staff are a school's most important asset and play a major part in determining its success.

In this chapter our findings on the sample schools' staffing are outlined. Attention is given to senior management, teachers, classroom assistants, residential social workers and ancillary staff as well as outside agencies giving support to the schools. The first part of the chapter is concerned with quantitative issues including length of service, gender and age balance, staff–pupil ratios, training, deployment and support systems. However, it is difficult to divorce the reporting of these findings from discussion of their impact and relationship to the quality of provision. Comment is therefore made on salient features which relate to the achievement and maintenance of proficiency and which help to separate effective schools from those identified as having serious weaknesses.

The latter sections of the chapter turn to the qualities perceived as relevant in the questionnaire and interview responses to effective teaching and care. What are the skills and personal traits of the adults who become 'significant others' to pupils with EBD? How are they able to manage behaviour which can be very challenging? How, to borrow the phrase of one of the interviewees, do they manage 'to switch on the switched off', and how do they have the resilience to create and sustain successful schools?

Length of service

In the light of the demanding nature of the work, one reason for the numbers of 'failing' schools might be rapid turnover of staff or difficulties in recruitment? For senior staff, is there a difficult initial period as they learn the ropes and then an optimum 'shelf life'? Mortimore *et al.* (1983) judged junior school headteachers to be at their most successful when they had been in their job between three and seven years, while those who had been in post for more than eleven years tended to become 'stale'. In the present study the periods during which headteachers had held their current appointments are summarised in Table 4.1. It can be seen that 55 per cent of the headteachers had been in post for more than five years, with just over half of these in post for over ten years.

Table 4.1 Time in post for headteachers, deputies and teachers

	Under 1 year %	1 to 2 years %	2 to 5 years %	5 to 10 years %	Over 10 years %	
Headteachers	15	10	20	27	28	n = 155
Deputy headteachers	21	11	24	31	13	n = 148
Other teachers	14	13	26	5 or more years 47%		n = 1158

On the basis of our visits and interviews we concur with the findings of mainstream effectiveness researchers and with the views of OFSTED that the headteacher is perhaps the most important single factor determining the success of a school (see Cole and Visser 1998). One factor in headteachers' effectiveness would appear to be the length of time they are in post, but once in post, status and salary often make it difficult for headteachers to move. In these circumstances it can be problematic if the philosophy and practice of the post holder does not keep abreast of developments in provision and criteria for successful practice. There can also be problems when long-serving headteachers have 'given their all' and are in danger of succumbing to the pressures of the job; our visits and interviews suggested that there are indeed very dedicated headteachers 'hanging in there'. On the other hand some headteachers approaching retirement were still innovatory in maintaining good practice but a common characteristic of their situations was that they were in larger schools where staffing levels permitted deputies and other staff to relieve them of some of the daily grind. We also noted how quickly new headteachers in their late thirties or early forties could turn round chaotic and apparently hopeless situations through strength of personality, energy and a contrasting philosophy to their predecessors. Finally, we were struck by the number of schools with acting headteachers as a result of the enforced or voluntary departure, or extended sick leave, of the permanent post holders. We know of one acting headteacher who has held this title for two years while his authority dallies over a new inclusive special needs policy.

Mortimore *et al.* (1983) stressed the key role played by deputy headteachers. We would concur with this assessment on the evidence of our visits. We were struck by the strength of the relationship between headteachers and their deputies in some of the good practice schools and how the natural propensities of one would complement the abilities of the other. Similarly, the ability of a new headteacher to appoint a competent and like-minded deputy early in his or her tenure would seem to be a crucial step in helping a struggling school to recover. Where a good working relationship had been forged the partnership might last for decades, helping to explain the long service of many deputies (see Table 4.1). However, as with headteachers, another reason for the long length of service of many deputies might be status and salary considerations.

The length of service of class teachers was also noteworthy. As can be seen in Table 4.1, 47 per cent had taught in the same school for over five years and a further 26 per cent for over two years. The authors' visits confirmed our impression that this is both a strength, contributing to stability, positive ethos and longevity of relationships but also a weakness with some staff, whose teaching abilities might not match OFSTED criteria or whose motivation may be lacking, remaining in jobs to the detriment of the school. It is possible for a teacher to have one year's experience twenty times over and to persevere with a model of teaching and meeting pupils' needs that is out of tune with expectations and requirements for good practice. Both employment law and the 'humanity' of headteachers and governing bodies often seem to help to keep in post staff whose effectiveness has become limited. On our visits to some schools where practice was uneven, headteachers were 'hanging on to the devil they knew' because experience indicated that better quality teachers would not be forthcoming were a vacancy to be created. We return later to recruitment difficulties in urban areas and also in rural locations where the bad reputation of a school locally, exacerbated by publicity surrounding a poor OFSTED report, makes recruitment difficult.

Our data also indicates that it is rare for newly qualified teachers to work in EBD schools. Three-quarters of the sample were reported as having more than ten years' teaching experience and 17 per cent between three and ten years. The comments of a one headteacher were of interest:

> 'I don't take on probationary teachers. You need experience. If you've had a bad day you've got to remember how you taught (other children) successfully.' [M036]

Quality of provision in residential schools is also clearly related to the experience, abilities and commitment of the care staff. Data from 63 schools in the sample gives a mean 'time in post' of 6.9 years for Heads of Care (HOC), with a number serving for over ten years and some for as many as 20. As with headteachers, many of these staff are likely to be at the pinnacle of their careers with practical incentives of high salary and, sometimes, subsidised housing inducing them to stay. The mean length of previous service as residential social workers (RSWs) is 9.6 years but promotion for able candidates can be swift, particularly in schools with only a small residential component. One HOC had only one and a half years' previous experience while 28 per cent had less than five. For Deputy Heads of Care (DOCs), nearly 26 per cent had had no previous experience as RSWs. A few had been teachers.

While time in post for DOCs ranged from a few months to 26 years, the mean was 6.6 years. As for senior teaching staff, some schools had very stable senior care staffing. It seems likely that their experience and longevity of service contributes to a school's positive ethos and helps to explain the praise given to some schools for their care arrangements by OFSTED when educational arrangements have been criticised.

Details were also obtained on 409 'middle ranking' and 376 'junior' Residential Child Care Officers. Many schools exhibited continuity of staffing for middle ranking staff as Table 4.2 demonstrates. However, providing residential education is costly and there is a tendency for the salaries of young junior care workers to be depressed to the point where recruitment is very difficult. In addition, the closure of many Children's Homes has reduced the pool of experienced staff from which to recruit and some independent schools, following the American intern model, choose to offer short-term contracts to, for example, young psychology graduates, as an experience-widening prelude to other careers. It is therefore perhaps not surprising that rates of turnover for junior staff, as evidenced in Table 4.2, are far higher for this group.

Table 4.2 Time in post for residential social workers

	Less than 1 year %	1 to 2 years %	3 to 5 years %	Over 5 years %	
Middle ranking	5	14	32	49	n = 409
Junior Residential Care Officers	29	27	22	22	n = 376

In summary, our interview and questionnaire data suggest that the successful EBD school has a stable nucleus of skilled, experienced and long-stay workers amounting to at least 30 per cent of their staffing establishment. They also manage to move on 'failing' staff to make possible the injection of 'new blood' and the creation of opportunities to adjust curriculum or styles of child care. Practice in highly rated schools can, as one headteacher reported to us, become 'stale and stilted' when senior or middle-ranking staff are 'seeing their time out'. These people were reported to side-step important issues and to look for easy short-term solutions which were not in the school's longer-term interests. The same headteacher lamented: 'We don't have the young guns now. They have moved on to be Heads of Units' [N04]. In other establishments it was evident that a new headteacher, who was able to bring in two or three highly competent and motivated teachers or experienced RSWs, over a couple of years could have a dramatic impact on the standards and stability of a school previously in difficulties.

Gender, age and race

According to Circular 11/90 (DES 1990) (the current government guidance on staffing for special educational needs) achieving a balance between female and male staff is important in creating a natural and healthy ethos in schools. Gender balance is necessary to cope with practical issues; for example, it is not possible for male staff to oversee girls going to bed at night. Equally, young people need to share their lives with staff of both sexes if they are to develop positive role models for both sexes. Desirable 'rough and tumble' play (Blatchford and Sharp 1994) or some types of sport might develop more naturally with male staff while Millham *et al.* (1975) noted a non-macho, female approach to control and motivation of difficult young men was often more effective. They joined Carlebach (1967) in noting the existence of too many militaristic, male-dominated regimes with all manner of poor practice. Dockar-Drysdale (1968), writing from a psychodynamic perspective, sees the need for warm, caring female staff who can be 'mother figures'. Further, the students' parents might find it easier to relate to different sexes.

However, only 15 per cent of headteachers in our study were women. The percentage at deputy headteacher level appears to be higher with a third of the good practice schools visited by us having female deputies. In 53 per cent of these 15 schools the gender balance of the headteacher and deputies was mixed while 47 per cent had an all male team. We did not encounter an all woman senior management team. Of 64 heads of care in the sample schools 31 per cent were women. The percentage rises to 42 per cent for the second most senior group of RSWs.

Information from open-ended replies in the care questionnaire indicated no salient features in relation to gender balance. Where there was an imbalance, usually towards women on the care side, senior staff expressed the desire to correct it – but given recruitment difficulties this was seen as difficult to achieve.

The fact that few teachers in EBD schools have under three years' teaching experience, suggests that young teachers do not gain posts in most of these schools. For care staff, we did elicit information on 832 RSWs.

Table 4.3 Age distribution of residential social workers in EBD schools (%)

Under 20 years %	20 to 25 years %	26 to 35 years %	36 to 50 years %	Over 50 years %	
0.5	16.5	45	31	7	n = 832

Table 4.3 suggests that care work with challenging youngsters would seem to be neither a teenager's, nor a middle-aged person's, job. We can only wonder on the nature of the escape routes of those care workers in their forties who leave the profession. We were told more than once that this was 'a younger person's game' and a deputy headteacher alluded to the need for an abundance of energy which allowed staff to run around and do things with the pupils rather than just talking to them.

The questionnaire did not probe the ethnicity of staff but at schools where there were pupils from minority ethnic groups, headteachers did show an awareness of the need to appoint more staff from ethnic minorities. Making such appointments was not always easy and not without its problems; one headteacher, for example, spoke of a Nigerian teacher encountering prolonged difficulty with British pupils of African-Caribbean origins. On the other hand, one school found the contribution of a visiting African-Caribbean counsellor of huge value, helping to offset the lack of teachers from ethnic minorities. Less positively, in the schools where there were few or no pupils from ethnic minority groups the fact that all of the staff were of white caucasian origin appeared to be of little concern. We note that very few staff (or pupils) of Asian origin were observed in the sample schools.

Staff–pupil ratios

At the time of writing, Circular 11/90 (DES 1990) constitutes the official guidance on this topic. Legal duties under Education Acts have to be met and for care in boarding schools there should be 'sufficient and suitable staff to ensure the proper care, supervision and welfare' outside the classroom (DES 1990, p. 4). However, particularly for teaching ratios, it warns that 'there can be no blueprint for ideal staffing arrangements in any educational institution' (p. 1). Nevertheless, it gives a tantalising but often unrealisable formula for pupils 'branded' as having serious emotional and behavioural difficulties. For these, there should be 0.15 of a teacher per pupil. This is another way of repeating the advice given in its precursor, Circular 4/73 (DES 1973), which suggested a ratio of one full-time teacher to every seven pupils. Optimistically, 11/90 advises the same ratio for special support assistants (SSAs) but requires a much smaller ratio for care staff: 'There should be sufficient staff to provide pupils with the same amount of access to adult time (i.e. teacher time plus SSA time) as there would be during school lessons.' The cost implications of this advice would seem to have precluded its implementation in many schools, particularly in relation to SSAs, and it is noteworthy that the OFSTED reports never refer in detail to this 'gold standard'. Heads, on our visits, referred to it wistfully, having found it a sword with a rather blunt edge when used to obtain additional resources from LEAs. The headteacher of one primary school, which was highly praised by OFSTED, noted that if Circular 11/90 was followed by his LEA, staffing costs would rise by 20 per cent.

Our findings revealed that the mean size of teaching group for core subjects was 7.4 pupils. However, in more than 15 per cent of the schools, pupils were taught in groups of nine and occasionally ten – class sizes found by Weaver (1968) over thirty years ago. At the other extreme some small independent schools provided groups of six or less. It was common for classes to number eight pupils.

Numbers of learning support assistants (LSA) hardly ever equalled the number of teachers. The mean was 4.5 per school. As the average school size was 46 pupils, there was commonly one LSA for every ten pupils rather than the suggested ratio of one to seven. This was reflected in the schools we visited where it was common for schools to be two or three LSAs short and sometimes for there to be half, or less, of the recommended number. The situation was sometimes worse when funding only allowed part-time appointments. Conversely, it could be better in some boarding schools where care staff assisted with some daytime education duties. A third of the 66 schools replying to the care questionnaire indicated that this happened in their establishment.

A headteacher where there were only five full-time equivalent SSAs for nine classes, said that he could manage fairly successfully when no teaching or LSA staff were away sick – but this is an infrequent occurrence in EBD schools.

When a school is also providing residential care, the pressures on senior staff are often intensified as senior staff are likely to be involved in providing cover in the evenings, and sometimes at weekends, in addition to their normal 'on call' care duties. The advice in Circular 11/90 would seem to imply a care staff–pupil ratio of about 1:3 or 1:4. Our sample showed that in nearly two thirds of schools the ratio was 1:5 or less. One to four was common and one to seven unusual. Ratios at peak times, for example, for early evening activity periods, are improved in 62.5 per cent of the sample schools by teachers performing evening care duties.

Quantity of staff does not necessarily equal quality of provision, as might be deduced from the reference to the school receiving a highly favourable OFSTED report despite a clear shortage of SSAs. Indeed, when we visited a school richly endowed with numbers of care staff and SSAs, the behaviour of the children was arguably the least controlled that we witnessed. Achieving low ratios is partly a function of deployment to which we turn next.

Deployment

The use of teaching staff in care hours no longer meets with the approval accorded it by the Underwood Committee (Ministry of Education 1955) or Dockar-Drysdale (1968) and is being consciously reduced by some headteachers who realise that it is relatively cheaper to employ more full-time RSWs. Furthermore, such duties are sometimes viewed as impacting negatively on teachers' performance in class and some Registered Inspectors have looked disapprovingly upon it in OFSTED reports, particularly where the traditional 15 hours are still being worked. Our data, based on returns from 37 schools, suggests that 15 hours was still the norm in about 40 per cent of schools while in a similar percentage of schools it was eight hours or less.

In another question, we were informed that in 22 per cent of schools teachers performed care duties only 'occasionally' and in 16 per cent of schools 'never'. Table 4.4 summarises the way in which teachers in those 22 per cent of schools are expected to contribute to care.

Table 4.4 Teachers' contribution to evening or weekend care (n = 54)

	Regularly %	Occasionally %	Never %
General care duties (e.g. putting children to bed)	57	30	13
Group activities in areas in which qualified	72	15	13
Group activities in areas in which interested	76	20	4
Teachers lead care teams	19	21	60

Extended hours for care workers were more common but this was usually based on care workers agreeing to put in longer hours in term time in exchange for the same holidays as teachers. This involves RSWs in many schools working between four and eight daytime hours a week. By working a 43 or 44 hour week it is then possible for RSWs to receive ten or 11 weeks' holidays instead of the five or six to which they would be entitled normally. This practice would seem to be widespread with the mean hours per week worked by RSWs in term time being 42.2 hours (sample size: 62 schools). In one school, RSWs were required to work an additional 15 hours (the traditional amount of 'extraneous duties' required of teachers) in exchange for an allowance. The financial inducement was claimed to make a 50-plus hour week acceptable.

Low pupil–staff ratios are of course made more difficult when teachers are allowed time away from the children for administration, meetings, reviews, etc. This space might be created by the headteacher or deputy taking on a teaching role; described as good practice by Circular 11/90, although it advises that the headteacher's input should not be counted against the school's teaching complement. Our data revealed that headteachers did indeed teach but rarely for more than a half day a week and the amount tends to decrease as the size of the school increases. For deputy headteachers the mean figure was 3.58 sessions per week (typically between a day and a half and two days a week). In smaller schools this could be substantially more and, on occasion, amounted to a full teaching timetable. In larger schools it was also common for senior teachers and middle-ranking teachers with additional responsibilities to be granted two or three additional sessions away from the classroom. For class teachers, it was usual for them to have a half-day a week available for administration and planning with one 'good practice' school creating as much as a day and a half a week. At the other extreme, another school offered its teachers no administration time and the teachers had opted to play an active role in both playtime and dinner duties on the basis that this aided control and fostered a more positive ethos. However, in this school the teaching day started at 9.30 a.m. and ended at 3 p.m. and thus it could be argued that the staff's administration and planning could take place at either end of the working day.

Circular 11/90 advised that the provision of administration time and chance for small group or individual counselling sessions should be permitted by staffing formulae, particularly for care staff. What this envisaged is not clear but that such advice should not be over-prescriptive and allow schools to evolve systems which suit their style of working and the particular needs of their establishment seems appropriate.

Match of teaching to training

A key issue in the deployment of human resources is the ability to match the subject being taught with subject specialists. The impact of this on pupils' responsiveness in class is discussed in Chapter 6. Table 4.5 shows that EBD schools seem to be well-endowed with some subject specialists and poorly with others. Subjects not mentioned in the table included Careers (14), Outdoor Education (5) and Psychology (3).

Table 4.5 Number of teachers professionally qualified or having undertaken substantial training in different subjects

English	210
PE	199
Science	166
Mathematics	130
Geography	130
Art	120
History	117
Design and Technology	101
General Primary	99
Music	47
Information Technology	42
Modern Foreign Languages	41
Drama	38
Home Economics	35

Difficulties in delivering the National Curriculum in modern foreign languages, music and technology are not surprising given the data in Table 4.5. Somewhat surprising was the finding that only 121 out of the 210 trained English teachers are actually delivering their specialist subject and that 125 teachers not trained to teach it (although a few had received general primary training) are required to do so. Have the trained English teachers become largely non-teaching members of the senior management teams (SMT) or are they versatile 'generalists' who perforce have to teach humanities, MFL or RE? In interviews, we heard evidence, particularly in the south-east, of the difficulties of recruiting specialists in less 'popular' subject areas. Suffice it to say here that our interview and questionnaire data suggest that headteachers preferred flexible curriculum generalists who were good at motivating EBD pupils ahead of teachers who were expert in a subject. One headteacher commented: 'It's no good having a subject specialism if you can't manage the children.' Another elaborated: 'The pure subject-oriented teachers would not be happy here. Teaching subjects to A level hasn't to be their *raison d'etre.*' The realities of running small special schools for challenging youngsters would seem to explain their preference. These were both headteachers of schools which had fared well in OFSTED inspections.

The presence of non-qualified teachers in our sample schools was rare although it should be noted that the use of instructors qualified, for example, in joinery, painting and decorating and bricklaying in one school seemed very effective with small groups of Year 10 and Year 11 students who went on to gain nationally recognised vocational qualifications.

Training for teachers

Cooper *et al.* (1991b) reported that 30 per cent of teachers in schools for EBD pupils had undertaken additional training. Answers in the present survey suggest a slightly higher figure of 36 per cent. Whether this apparent increase will be maintained seems unlikely in the light of answers to a different question in which over 46 per cent of respondents indicated that no member of their staff had been funded to attend a long, award bearing EBD or SEN course since September 1993. The exceptions were one school which claimed 20 and another ten. Most schools reported between one and three. Of the schools visited by the authors one claimed five while another, which has been consistently held up as an exemplar of good practice by OFSTED and HMI, reported none. But in the latter, four members of the senior management team had achieved additional qualifications prior to 1993. However, the question is raised whether the leaders of EBD schools of tomorrow are being given sufficient training?

Respondents were asked to nominate long and short courses which they would recommend. Unfortunately a disappointing response was received with only a few nominations for unspecific counselling courses, for the University of Birmingham specialist diploma and degree courses, for courses in specific learning difficulties and general special educational needs and the study skills courses and conferences of the Association of Workers for Children with Emotional and Behaviour Difficulties (AWCEBD). Short courses on Attention Deficit Hyperactivity Disorder (ADHD), Assertive Discipline and child protection were also mentioned. On the authors' visits to schools, it was established that various schools had 'bought in' training in physical restraint techniques from independent trainers. There was also a tendency to recommend the courses offered by a school's local university; geographic proximity facilitating access to 'twilight learning' seen perhaps as an advantage. Short and day courses, occasionally offered by a school's local LEA advisory service, were identified in contrasting numbers by different schools.

In sum, the verdict of one questionnaire respondent would seem to reflect the view of many when he wrote: 'Acute staffing difficulties, difficulty of supply cover and OFSTED inspection severely limit INSET'. There was also the suspicion that some senior managers were suspicious of the value of the training on offer, preferring a policy of 'grow your own'. The patchy and less than satisfactory situation in regard to staff training painted by HMI (DES 1989b) would still seem to apply.

Training of non-teachers

HMI (DES 1989b) had been particularly concerned about the induction and the continuing development of non-teaching staff. This was therefore another important area to probe. In the questionnaire, 48 per cent of classroom assistants were reported to have received relevant training, although details were not given on the courses undertaken and some of it may have been short or part-time.

For Heads of Care our data suggest a figure of at least 51 per cent claiming to have a professional qualification. As some respondents chose not to answer this question this percentage must be treated with care. The most common courses were the now defunct Certificate of Social Services (CSS), followed by the similarly defunct Certificate of Qualification in Social Work (CQSW) and then by teaching certificates. Only 4 per cent had acquired the current standard qualification, the Diploma in Social Work (DipSW). On a qualitative note, the old CSS was rated as 'very relevant' by 12 out of 21 respondents (57 per cent) compared to seven out of 19 (37 per cent) describing the DipSW in similar terms. There were many calls in the open-ended questions for a nationally recognised qualification which specialised in residential child care. The demise of the Certificate in the Residential Care of Children and Young People (CRCCYP), in which some older HOCs were qualified, was remembered with affection. Although they are viewed as being of value as basic qualifications, the shortcomings and difficulties of achieving NVQ Levels 2 and 3 were noted by some of our respondents.

More highly rated were diplomas and certificates in counselling skills (undertaken by about 15 per cent of the sample) and for a small number of people who had undertaken it the Open University course, 'Working with Children and Young People'. Six RSWs were reported to have taken the AWCEBD certificate courses, the majority of respondents seeing these as very relevant.

When respondents were asked to nominate useful in-house or short-course training a predictable array of subjects was suggested, including behaviour management (specifically dealing with aggression, anger management, control and restraint); child protection issues; and school procedures such as record keeping. Those advocating a minimalist and highly practical approach, suggested that staff would benefit from regular day visits to similar establishments to observe practice and copy ideas.

Our data suggest a severe, and perhaps worsening, situation with regard to meeting RSWs' training needs, particularly in regard to long-term, award bearing courses. Financial stringency makes the freeing up of time for any substantial course a rare event in most schools and even if money is found for cover, what is on offer? The evolution of a more challenging Level 4 NVQ, promised now for almost a decade, has been lamentably slow in appearing. Further, doubts exist about its likely relevance to the care of challenging children. Some older hands indicated they prefer the reinstatement of a dedicated nationally recognised course other than NVQ about whose currency they have doubts. One or two would prefer courses to be provided at colleges, while others wanted them delivered in the main at the RSWs' place of work. The situation for in-house training for care staff seemed variable in quantity and quality.

Staff development in many schools was often kept within the school and restricted to induction by experienced staff, followed by informal guidance; for RSWs it could take the form of supervision. In an ideal situation every member of staff would have time allocated to sit down with a senior and respected fellow professional, preferably not their line manager, and have the opportunity for open and uninterrupted discussions about their professional performance with the supervisor listening and making suggestions to help the supervisee (Pettes 1979). It might extend to the supervisee being observed in action in their normal work. Frequency would relate to need: for new staff it would perhaps be timetabled every week, while for experienced staff perhaps once each half term. Support systems were said to be in place in 50 of the 66 schools replying to the care questionnaire, although information could not be gathered on the details of these systems. Nevertheless, 59 per cent of the respondents claimed it helped care staff's professional development 'a great deal' and a further 37 per cent 'somewhat'. Similarly 60 per cent claimed it helped to ease stress and to relieve the pressures of RSWs' jobs 'a great deal' and 40 per cent somewhat.

About 60 per cent of schools also operated an appraisal system. The data is insufficient to say whether these were meaningful and helpful or as perfunctory as some of the systems reported in the main questionnaire for teachers; in some schools, the latter might only receive an appraisal interview once every two or three years. We were left with a clear impression that appraisal was being carried out in some schools because it was now required, rather than because the school saw it as useful. Operating appraisal systems is a function of management and further discussion of this topic is left to the next chapter.

The contribution of other support staff

The word 'ancillary' is avoided as it is described in the Concise Oxford Dictionary as 'subservient or subordinate', deriving from the Latin for handmaid. While on diagrams of school staffing structures, part-time therapists, secretaries, nurses, caretakers, cooks, dinner supervisors and laundry and other domestic assistants will appear at the bottom of management trees, this is not how they are regarded or used in the good practice schools. They often possess expertise lacking in teaching and care staff; one headteacher spoke with relief of the facility of an administrative assistant in operating spreadsheets and financial planning – without her, LMSS would have seemed impossible. For such support staff there should be clarity of role definition but this should not become a constricting demarcation which precludes their ability to make the valuable contribution we observed in our good practice schools. These people will have been chosen with care and can form warm, supportive relationships with children, showing empathy and involving children in worthwhile social activity as successfully as some teachers or care workers do. It is the little things in life in EBD schools which often make the difference between a positive ethos and an atmosphere of mistrust and confrontation. Cooks prepare meals, nurses administer medicine, secretaries receive messages from teachers via pupils in their office but it is how the support staff interact with the children and their parents which make a difference.

The questionnaire returns did not produce data on the quantity of support staff and the above comments reflect observations made on visits to good practice schools. Proficiency does require sufficient administration, domestic, maintenance and nursing staffing. Our observations suggested some schools were better endowed in this respect than others. We observed in some schools staff who might be perceived as acting outside their roles as they would be perceived in a mainstream school but they displayed understanding of how to cope with difficult behaviour and were clearly being encouraged by management to make a positive contribution to the wider life of the school. In one residential school, for example, as part of their daily duties, the maintenance officers acted as waiters in the school dining room. At a KS3 EBD school, with only three classes, the secretary was a former psychiatric nurse who was observed giving emotional, as well as physical, first aid as she extracted the gravel from a child's grazed knee; she was at the very hub of that school's life and seen as a 'significant other', caring and comforting yet strict and given respect by many of the pupils. As she put it to one of the authors:

'It's all about people. We like the children. We're good at negotiation. Discipline is by relationships. You can't be dogmatic or bang desks.'

At the same school, the headteacher described his long search for a suitable site manager and how pleased he was to have found the present incumbent who took small groups of children for photography sessions and involved them in maintenance tasks as part of their technology programmes. In another school, an hour after an obstreperous and tipsy day pupil had been bundled off the site by the headteacher, the youngster was observed lapping up the emotional first aid on offer from the handyman who had allowed him to help fix a trellis to the front of the school. At another school a cook had become a RSW and assisted with the decorating of care units with the children helping. Finally, by way of example, the part-time speech therapist at another school was accompanying a class on an outdoor pursuits trip on the day of our visit, commenting later in interview, that this really helped her to get to know the children and form relationships.

In summary, the support staff in good schools will be present in sufficient numbers but will also be a respected part of the overall staff team and encouraged to interact with the pupils. They will share the sense of 'ownership' of the school that should permeate the teaching and care staff.

Governors

After the distribution of the national survey forms, the authors received a heartfelt letter from a governor of one school pointing out that their role had not been acknowledged in any shape or form. This apparent oversight was corrected by other means and in the course of the school visits we met governors who were invited by the headteacher or chose to be present. Besides responsibilities required by Education Acts, the contributions made by governors can be divided into the following areas.

- *Advocates for the school in relation to the LEA*. Effective governors were reported as being useful allies in relations with LEAs – for example, in the battle for resources and also sometimes in making the case for the continuing status quo of a school. One Chair of governors, who was a dentist, was active in preventing the LEA 'dumping' a mobile classroom in the playground and creating a disaffection unit in a successful primary EBD school. Another actively fought for the continuance of a residential school, threatened with closure after chronic management problems and a highly critical OFSTED report.
- *Advocates for the school in relation to the local community*. One governor, a former secondary headteacher, recounted how he conducted a successful PR campaign in support of a new headteacher appointed after the previous incumbent had largely lost control of the behaviour of the students which had led to damaged relations with the well-to-do neighbourhood.
- *Ally of the headteacher in relation to parents*. Headteachers can find it useful to have a governor alongside them when dealing with parents in fraught situations, e.g. in connection with exclusions or readmittance of children.
- *Ally of the headteacher in relation to the staff*. We heard of one governor entering the staff room on a regular basis and being around the school, reinforcing the messages the headteacher was trying to get across.

- *Confidante and supporter of the headteacher.* In the lonely and exposed position of headteacher, it is invaluable to have someone not on the staff to whom the headteacher can talk about difficult issues and on whom ideas can be tried out. Our visits offered some evidence that a trusted governor sometimes acted in this role.

In 'good practice' schools headteachers clearly find their governing bodies a major support, speaking highly of the time and commitment put in by them for little public reward or recognition.

Support given by external agencies

In their study of 47 EBD schools between 1983 and 1988, HMI (DES 1989b) found contrasting situations with regard to the quantity and quality of support offered by LEA and health services. Somewhat surprisingly the contribution of social services was not reported. By far the most frequent help was given by educational psychologists. Trailing far behind in second place were LEA special education or curriculum advisers giving regular assistance. These were followed by education welfare officers, psychiatrists and a few mentions for nurses, general practitioners, speech or other therapists and child guidance workers. In 47 per cent of the HMI sample the quality of the overall support of these professionals was rated as 'good', in 17 per cent 'adequate' and in 36 per cent 'poor/non-existent'.

Our survey asked schools to rate the quantity of input from external agencies on a four-point scale from 'extensive' through 'regular' and 'some' to 'little'. For quality, they were asked to rate it as 'excellent', 'good', 'fair' or 'poor'. We are aware that only a 'broad brush' subjective sketch is being offered. However it represents accurately the *perceptions* of the schools on these matters.

- *Educational psychologists.* The most commonly used agency was the educational psychology service. Echoing Smith and Thomas' (1993b) findings for 1988, input falls far short of being 'regular' in many parts of the country. Only four respondents (2.5 per cent), three of whom were from independent establishments, reported 'extensive' support; 40.5 per cent said 'regular'; 35 per cent 'some'; and 22 per cent 'little'. Twenty-one schools (14 per cent) rated the quality of support as 'excellent'; 37 per cent as 'good'; 35 per cent as 'fair'; and only 14 per cent as 'poor'.
- *Field social workers.* Continuing exhortations to closer inter-agency working would seem to be well-founded in the light of our findings

in relation to field social workers. Only 5 per cent of our sample reported 'extensive' support; 19 per cent said 'regular'; 40 per cent 'some'; and 36 per cent 'little'. More worrying than the lack of quantity was the fact that only 2.5 per cent of respondents assessed the quality of support as 'excellent'; 12.5 per cent as 'good'; while as many as 30 per cent said 'poor'.

- *Educational Social Workers (ESW) attached to school/Educational Welfare Officer (EWO)*. Eighty-seven schools reported input from ESWs attached to their school with mean quantity close to 'some'. Seventy-four schools reported input from EWOs but with only 8 per cent saying it is 'extensive'; the mean rating is between 'some' and 'regular'. The quality of input can be summarised for ESWs attached to schools as between 'fair' and 'good' while for the EWOs, slightly closer overall to 'good'.

- *Input from mental health professionals*. The extent of psychiatric input was rated overall as being between 'little' and 'some', with no school saying that it was 'extensive'. Fifty-nine per cent said it amounted to 'little'. Only eight respondents mentioned psychotherapists and half that number mentioned psychiatric social workers (PSWs). This is perhaps to be expected when headteachers do not see children with severe psychiatric difficulties as falling within their purview (see Chapter 3). However, the survey reports a situation which is different from Weaver's (1968) findings in an era when Child Guidance Clinics played a more prominent role. Weaver found that more psychiatrists than educational psychologists visited schools for the maladjusted and PSWs were active in more schools. Seven per cent of our respondents rated the input of psychiatrists as 'excellent', with the mean being very close to 'fair'. The few psychotherapists were quite highly rated.

In the open-ended section of this question the following professions were mentioned: nurse (19 nominations); speech therapist (10); counsellor (8); careers officer (7); GP (7); LEA advisors (7); physiotherapist (7); police liaison or other officers (7). There were five or less mentions for schools medical officers, clinical psychologists, behaviour support services, child protection officers and only three for LEA officers. If the responses are accurate the low level of input from LEA officers and special education advisers is surprising although it does link with the implicit criticism of many LEAs for 'failing' schools in OFSTED reports. There are rare (often single) mentions for other professions; for example, one for a homeopath and one for a music therapist. Quantity of input from these 'other professions' rarely reaches 'regular'.

On the qualitative scale clinical psychologists and police liaison emerge on top. Sadly, given the possible links between language difficulties and EBD claimed more than once by senior staff at the good practice schools, only two out of eight speech therapists were rated as either 'excellent' or 'good'.

The personal qualities of effective workers with children with EBD

It has been claimed for some decades in both the USA and in the UK that effective work with children with EBD depends heavily on the experience, personalities and value systems of those employed to work with them. Fritz Redl noted in an article first drafted in 1939 that a sense of humour was 'the most vital characteristic of the skilful handler of discipline problems', that 'false dignity' tended to produce 'confusion, uproar and mismanagement' and that the attitudes and feelings of staff were 'powerful milieu ingredients':

> I mean the attitudes and feelings that really fill the place, that are lived – not those that are only mentioned in research interviews and on questionnaires. (Redl 1966, p. 86)

He had written in the same article:

> The fact is that the youngsters not only respond to what we say . . . they also smell our value feelings even when we don't notice our own body odour any more. (p. 83)

Less colourfully, the Underwood Committee wrote in 1955:

> Experience is a good instructor, and the right qualities of character and personality are essential; no training however thorough can be a substitute for them. (p. 122)

Dawson (1980) made the same point, while Reid (1986) stressed the need for teachers to be able to make the disaffected feel wanted. Reinert and Huang (1987), while claiming that American teachers with 'children in conflict' were required to demonstrate essentially the same skills as those employed by 'good regular classroom teachers', stressed the extra effort needed, often outside normal teaching times, in terms of commitment to planning and acting as suitable role models. Galloway (1990) and Smith and Laslett (1993) are examples of more recent British writers pointing to the power of staff value systems and approaches, describing the capacity of staff in schools to both increase and to minimise the emotional and behavioural difficulties of their children. Cooper *et al.* (1994) stress the importance of teacher style and approach. So what did the senior staff in EBD schools think about this vital topic?

An open-ended question in the main questionnaire produced a wealth of evidence which, conscious of Redl's reservations about questionnaire answers, we cross-referenced to answers given to other questions made, for example by Heads of Care on the supplementary questionnaire as well as to data gathered in interviews. In the latter, we made a point of asking a range of key personnel about the qualities they looked for when appointing staff. Interestingly, many beliefs about the traits of a good teacher of children with EBD apply equally to good RSWs and to other support staff. The variables suggested by respondents and interviewees relate not so much to specialist subject knowledge or academic and theoretical training but rather to basic aspects of character, energy and degree of commitment, although mixed of course with at least a modicum of expertise. Our actual observations of practice in the best schools suggested that what staff described actually occurred in abundance in a variety of situations, from breakfast time through to 'lights out'.

The following descriptors received between five and three nominations each: respectful; good lesson pace; charisma; humble; acceptance of pupils; reliable; enthusiastic; emotional strength and stability; presentation skills; direct; sensible; 'hands on'.

The frameworks for inspection for primary, secondary and special schools (OFSTED 1995b, c and d) do not identify separate criteria for judging the quality of teaching in special schools. The OFSTED view would seem to be that a good teacher is a good teacher anywhere. Was this view echoed in the sample schools?

Respondents were asked in an open-ended question to describe the skills and traits of the teachers in their school which distinguished these staff from good mainstream practitioners. A few answered simply 'No', and others offered longer comments which agreed with the OFSTED view. One headteacher said that in theory this should be so but in practice the good EBD teacher had 'a spark which turns the ordinary teacher into a very good teacher'. The quotations below add to this but first is one headteacher's comment, representing many and reinforcing the most mentioned trait in Table 4.6.

'Organisation is the key.' [M211]

'Staff who are secure in themselves, have a good sense of humour, good team and individual players, persistent, enjoy a challenge, easily forgive, flexible and determined.' [M054]

Table 4.6 Rank order of characteristics of teaching style for effective teachers of children with EBD

	Nominations	*Per cent*
1 Good planning (49); well organised (34); structured (4)	87	56.1
2 Consistency (37); fairness (23)	60	39.7
3 Good sense of humour	56	36.1
4 Enthusiasm (31); interesting/challenging (6); passionate (5); stimulating (3)	45	29.0
5 Understanding individual needs (23); understanding EBD (13); knowledge of EBD (4); pupil knowledge (2)	42	27.1
6 Adaptability/flexibility	37	23.9
7 Empathy	29	18.7
8 Patience	28	18.1
9 Ability to form positive relationships with children	27	17.4
10 Gives positive reinforcement (12); stresses success (5); praises (5); encouraging (4)	26	16.8
11 = Good subject knowledge	25	16.1
Firmness (20); stubborn (5)	25	16.1
13 Calmness, relaxed, good humour	22	14.2
14 Uses a variety of responses/eclectic	20	12.9
15 = Has high expectations of pupils	19	12.3
Resilient (14); stamina (5)	19	12.3
17 Positive regard for/likes children with EBD (13); interested in pupils (5)	18	11.6
18 Carefully differentiates work	16	10.3
19 Sets clear boundaries	13	8.4
20 Skilled in behaviour management (7); effective discipline (5)	12	7.7
21 = Confident	11	7.1
Positive	11	7.1
23 = Caring	10	6.4
Tolerant	10	6.4
25 = Clarity of purpose	8	5.2
Determined	8	5.2
Team member	8	5.2
Honest	8	5.2
29 Experience of mainstream as well as EBD	6	3.9

'My folks have to have a strong internal locus of control.' [M196]

'The ability to take knocks to ego and come back for more. A broad back and a mental toughness. The ability to see positive traits in the youngsters. Not to be black/white, to have flexibility to put in steps to prevent youngsters from losing self-esteem.' [M084]

'Think quickly, act slowly. Relaxed manner – but firm.' [M149]

'Always accepting and welcoming of child unconditionally. Always looking to praise and be positive even with the most negative, destructive and abusive children (not easy!).' [M030]

The same headteacher had also commented that staff should be 'non-judgemental – able to distinguish behaviour from the child'. This comment should be contrasted with a statement made in answer to another question where a headteacher agreed only with the second part of this statement. Reflecting the practice which we observed and heard described to us, he saw it as:

'important to be *judgmental* but without *rejecting* the child'. [N12].

Another argued that staff should have:

'The ability to depersonalise behaviour, i.e. to see behaviour as a symptom of a wider problem rather than an attack on one's personality or ability.' [M175]

There now follow three comments indicating that it is appreciated that staff need professional knowledge and understanding of the nature of their clientele. One stressed the importance of 'Presenting in well-planned small steps and making as many things practical/hands on as possible' [M210]. Another talked of the 'Ability to spot potential flashpoints and defuse situations before behaviour becomes extreme' [M069]. A senior staff member in a therapeutic community talked of the need for 'understanding of psychodynamic processes' [R21]. This was a rare usage of the word 'psychodynamic'.

Sometimes it was suggested that a tinge of 'EBD' in the personalities or experiences of the staff in their own lives helps. The respondent from a small registered independent ventured 'Mildly deviant behaviour?' Comments of this ilk were sometimes linked to references to the frequently mentioned 'sense of humour'. Is this a trite phrase which trips off people's tongues or is it an important aspect of working with children with EBD? It would seem to be viewed both as a mechanism for the release of pent-up stress and assistance in maintaining enthusiasm but also as a means of diverting pupil anger, turning around threatening situations and building and maintaining relationships. Observations during the school visits provided some evidence for both these perspectives. When we asked an IT teacher with twenty-five years' experience in the EBD schools about 'shelf-life' he replied unhesitatingly that it was his sense of humour which kept him going. We listened to the banter between staff: the headteacher of a southern school who believed in a no-nonsense, behaviourist approach ribbed his deputy for her sympathy for a more psychodynamic, counselling style. We observed the fun between many RSWs and teachers and pupils: when a child burst into a London headteacher's office as we talked to him the exchange went like this:

Pupil: 'Where's T?'
Head: 'I've eaten him.'
Pupil: 'Where is he?'
Head: 'What are you? A copper?'

At another school a Year 9 pupil, smartly dressed in a brand new uniform is about to be re-included into a mainstream secondary school. At morning assembly, the headteacher holds him up as an example for others to follow, wishes him well and hopes he will come back to visit his old school. At this point the deputy headteacher sitting in the body of the pupils calls out 'No thanks!' The joke is enjoyed by the child. We heard gentle humour used naturally and skilfully in the admonishing of pupils. A child who is arguing and shouting in the corridor at lesson changeover meets the headteacher who says to the children around the guilty party: 'Ian must have the loudest voice in the south of England'. The headteacher then looked directly at Ian and they exchange smiles as the boy goes quiet.

Another headteacher stressed not only humour but staff displaying *good* humour:

'Every time I drive up to school I have to get into smile mode. That's what it's all about.'

By displaying bad humour and shouting at children he claimed he could reduce the school to chaos in twenty minutes. The standard comment of a headmistress when presented with a new problem was 'It's all a laugh, in't?', typifying her staunch determination to see through any adversity with good humour and to see the 'funny side'.

These characteristics were often enhanced by a high degree of selflessness, captured in the following comments about teacher effectiveness:

'Ability to give, give, give and receive little in return.' [M095]

'You can't play at caring. You either do or you don't. Your can't just walk away at 3 p.m.' [M051]

It was common for the headteachers of the 'good practice schools' to sing the praises of their staff. A headteacher described his as 'people who would lie down in front of trucks for you.' Another described the qualities of a science teacher whose lesson we had just observed: 'She gives so much of herself to them' – often in her free time for science and gardening competitions in which her classes had been successful. As the authors made to leave one school, the headteacher opened her door to a member of staff who reported that a RSW, who had collapsed mid-evening while on duty at the swimming baths with the pupils the previous week, still needed to be persuaded to put the removal of her gall bladder ahead of going away on a school residential trip. The senior teacher at another school described the end-product of his dedication:

'It's more draining to give 50 per cent than 150. If I stuck to PE and history, I'd get nowhere. It's about being here for the kids . . . you give of yourself and the boys see you give . . . when they see that you are there to enable *them* to succeed, you are there.' [M158]

A few replies to the care questionnaire added to the picture of effective care staff. They adopted a genuine, child-centred approach, were good listeners and liked working with difficult children as well as being well organised and determined. They, as much as the effective teachers, tended to be self-deprecating, lacking 'side', committed and good at displaying an unruffled confidence, even when they might not have felt it. From conversations with various pupils on the school visits it would seem that the pupils' views on staff effectiveness mirrored the picture we have tried to sketch.

Before finishing this chapter, it is perhaps wise to add some balance to this extremely positive picture. The pupils to whom we spoke did refer to a lack of consistency, fairness and understanding in some staff. A Year 11 boy, holding forth in the headteacher's office and seated in the headteacher's chair as its normal recumbent sat at the other side of the meeting table, recounted his progression through four EBD schools, from over-permissive to unsympathetic regimes before his present placement, where he still encountered teachers who would 'bite back' or those who could bruise damaged egos by blunt comment. Some critical comments were also given in the questionnaire responses and in headteachers' assessment of their staff or those observed in other schools. One respondent wished to get away from the unhelpful and limiting 'cult of the EBD teacher', while a headteacher talked of refugee teachers from the mainstream going into EBD schools in the belief that they could escape from planning lessons and timetables. Another respondent saw the EBD teacher as 'idiosyncratic, odd and unusual'. One Head of Care viewed his place of work with pessimistic realism: 'We allow adults who want a job more than they want to do this job to remain in post.'

These comments are included to stress that the authors do not wish to paint a picture of unbridled altruism and self-sacrifice. OFSTED's criticisms of standards relating to ethos and behaviour as well as to the education provided in many schools cannot be brushed to one side. Indeed, on the visits to 'good practice' schools we encountered and observed senior staff struggling to improve the performance of some teachers and care workers and sometimes being forced to endure ingrained poor practice. How they went about these tasks is reflected in the content of the next chapter.

Chapter 5

Some Aspects of Management

A clear message from the OFSTED reports and from our data is that effective schooling for pupils with EBD depends heavily on the values, vision and energy of the headteacher and senior colleagues. The senior management of proficient schools display impressive interpersonal and organisational skills and are responsive to the demands and expectations of the world beyond their school gates. This chapter therefore focuses on some important aspects of management. First the nature of leadership in a proficient school is sketched. This is followed by comments on the value of written school documentation with a particular focus on school development plans (SDPs). The next section offers some reflections in the light of the authors' data on senior staff's responses to LMSS, the OFSTED inspection process and issues surrounding the 1989 Children Act. The penultimate section deals with how schools approach their work with pupils' parents and the final one on how senior managers assist staff's own 'survival' and development needs.

Effective leadership

Creating the proficient school calls for skill and commitment in abundance from senior staff but particularly from the headteacher. We endorse the message of the schools' effectiveness literature (e.g. Mortimore *et al.* 1983, Stoll 1991) on the need for high quality leadership from the headteacher. A noticeable feature of favourable OFSTED reports is the importance attached to the quality of headship with adjectives such as 'good', 'caring' and 'committed' and short phrases about 'vision' appearing. We also agree with the Scottish HMI's view that the 'inspiration, direction and support' offered by a headteacher is a reliable indicator of desirable ethos (Scottish Office Education Department 1992). We also subscribe to the view of Mortimore *et al.* (1983) that the assistance of an able deputy headteacher is of great importance for long-term effectiveness. To this we would add, for the residential school, that at least one other senior manager, usually the Head of Care, needs to be of high calibre. Finally, in these days of LMSS, financial planning needs to be undertaken by a fourth person if the traditional triumvirate, identified above, is to be able to devote its energies to its many other tasks. One of the early demands a headteacher, drafted in to rescue a school in special measures, made of his LEA was for the loan of a spreadsheet-literate administrative assistant from County Hall.

Sketched below is the nature of successful headship as suggested by our research data and the processes through which deputy headteachers and Heads of Care establish and legitimate their authority. Observations made on visits are neatly summarised by an advertisement, now incorporated into the job description, for the headteacher of one of the 'good practice' schools:

It is expected that the Head will:

- lead with decisiveness, clarity and vision, translating agreed aims into good practice

- be able to enthuse and motivate others

- be able to manage existing people and resources to good effect

- set high expectations for pupils and staff

- have a keen interest in the quality of teaching and learning in the school based on a proven record of effective teaching of children with emotional and behavioural difficulties

- be efficient, adaptable and well organised without making heavy weather of administration

- be able to forge positive links with parents, the local community and other schools in the area

- be sympathetic to and realistic in planning and delivering a suitable curriculum to children with emotional behavioural difficulties

In general we encountered headteachers realising these expectations and operating with their deputies and Heads of Care in the mould of consultative, responsive leadership advised by government (DES 1987, OFSTED 1993) and writers on 'effective schools' (e.g. Mortimore *et al.* 1983).

Most displayed a penchant for direct involvement with the pupils. They were observed attending breakfast, taking assemblies and getting into classes when possible. After thirteen years in post one headteacher chose to continue with two evening care duties a week, not as a distant 'on call' consultant but working in the front-line under a RSW team leader. Other headteachers also opted to continue with evening duties in order to have an up-to-date view of their school outside normal teaching times.

Members of SMTs were generally personable people, displaying the requisite character traits outlined in the last chapter in abundance. They develop warm, caring relationships, listen to staff and pupils, and foster the 'ownership', by both adults and children, of the systems for running their schools. But this never amounted to a fuzzy, laissez-faire liberalism; it was within their own chosen parameters. Amos (1997) talked of the need to provide 'rubber boundaries' for pupils with EBD. There should be order and clear direction for children but brought about in a flexible way, allowing for individual need; in other words schools should not operate in a rigid fashion. The 'rubber boundary' notion will be developed in relation to pupils in the next chapter, but it did also seem to guide our headteachers' approaches to the management task. One said he wanted staff to 'run with their ideas' and encouraged his new deputy to develop his own style. A headteacher of a large school compared his job as a new appointee in the mid 1980s with what he did now; having developed the school as he wanted it, he was happy that many of the tasks he used to perform were now carried out by middle managers, operating to some extent in their way but within his, and his long-stay, like-minded Head of Care's, limits. But he remained there to give support, to reinforce boundaries for the children and to lead by example. He was observed assisting in the control and counselling of pupils in support of colleagues, not 'behind the lines' in his office, but in full view of other staff and pupils. When the difficult or unexpected occurs it is incumbent upon headteachers to become personally involved, sometimes to go where angels fear to tread. When at a formal morning assembly, 60 pupils failed to join in a new hymn, it was the headteacher who emerged from the back of the chapel to take over, organise an impromptu practice and within five minutes had turned an embarrassing, snigger-ridden debacle into a zestful rendition – though his own uncertain baritone was more suited to Covent Garden market than the opera house.

Observation of senior staff in effective schools suggested that they were not afraid to intervene at selected moments, issuing injunctions and expecting the compliance of staff (and usually getting it because their management had won the respect of colleagues). SMTs had apparently proved their ability to deal with the most difficult children and their families. In reviving a school after a damning HMI report, one headteacher recounted how, in order to win back control for the staff over the pupils, he would stay with day pupils held back for detention well into the evening before personally running the children home and discussing the difficulties with their parents.

Determination mixed with skill and good organisation appeared to help win many difficult battles for the members of SMTs. These victories were observed by assistant staff; they were also seen by the pupils who would then pass on the message to new entrants. This served to legitimate their power within their school and the successful SMT exuded a relaxed authority which provided stability and security for staff and pupils alike. The most striking example was the observation of two male staff physically restraining a screaming and flailing child in the main corridor of a school. The boy was 'assisted' into an ante-room as a colleague called for the headteacher's assistance. We watched as after a very short period she quietly led the now tranquil child out of the room, gently holding his hand.

For this headteacher, achieving this position had probably been gradual. Later she confided that at times she felt she had to be very 'up-front', giving pupils loud 'rollickings' when confronting unacceptable behaviour – proving she could do this to pupils and to a staff who remembered the 'good old days' of her male predecessor who had adopted a more domineering and 'macho' style in disciplining pupils. This had helped establish her present authority which now usually allowed her to support staff in a relaxed manner while showing plenty of warmth and affection.

Once they had established their authority, headteachers said they could become more consultative and democratic but clear parameters for the staff and pupils had to be created first. It was noticeable that headteachers appointed to 'clear up' and revitalise schools which were in difficulties did not 'indulge' in democracy or give power to alienated, indifferent or 'burnt-out' staff. In most cases of this kind, existing staff cannot be replaced in the short or medium term and the new headteacher has to work with them and help as many as possible to rediscover their fire and develop effectiveness. One headteacher appointed to a residential school in special measures made a point of talking and listening to every member of staff before he formally took up his post. He also invited parents to a specially convened meeting at County Hall. But there, in the medium term at least, the democracy ended; in the three training days before the new term started, he issued written guidelines and explained exactly what the rules were for pupils and for staff. These were essentially his rules, bending only slightly to the wishes of many of the staff. This was followed by a period of a highly interventionist style in which he ensured that his standards and expectations would apply and that his writ would run throughout the school. In this, and other establishments, control of the pupils was a first priority, involving confrontations, where necessary, determined physical restraints and usually the exclusion of a few pupils whose extreme behaviour continued to undermine the desired ethos. The drift and disorganisation resulting from the previous regime which had induced low staff morale and fanned the embers of pupil disaffection had to be exorcised as swiftly as possible. A dose of autocracy was deemed essential as new systems were introduced. Another headteacher reported that when he took over his school, the staff were so used to daily disruption and bad behaviour that they just did not believe that the pupils could behave in a normal fashion, that lessons could be orderly and mealtimes controlled and relatively peaceful. Teachers and care staff had to be shown by his personal determination and example that their pessimism and low expectations were ill-founded.

One chair of governors described how his appointee turned round defeatist attitudes amongst the staff of a non-maintained school who were convinced that closure was imminent. One of the new headteacher's earliest actions, with the support of his chairman, was to announce that a substantial fund of money, which staff had expected might be available to support redundancy packages, would be spent on an extensive physical refurbishment package. These plans were carried out as part of a detailed plan for the long-term future. Within three years numbers on roll had risen from under 30 to over 70 and the governor and headteacher reported a revitalised staff.

Significantly however, in this and in other cases, the headteacher had, within a year, been able to bring in a new deputy. The latter shared the 'can-do' attitude (NCE 1996) of the headteacher but concentrated on curriculum development, thus freeing the headteacher to attend to wider and perhaps more fundamental issues (see the next section). The departure of other middle-ranking staff created openings for further infusions of new blood or promotions from within. The headteacher had not had to force these vacancies; elsewhere headteachers did have to. One spoke frankly, saying he had to be a 'hard-nosed and manipulative' manager; it was necessary to 'manoeuvre around', eventually persuading some staff to admit to themselves that they were failing and that their future lay elsewhere.

In all the above instances, the end was clear – the welfare of the school and the benefit of the pupils. The means were various; sometimes the headteachers' verbal facility was a powerful and sufficient tool but sometimes unconventional, or financial, wheeling and dealing with individuals, local community and LEAs was necessary.

Visits by the authors suggested that the calmest schools with the best motivated, highest achieving pupils were those with pragmatic, eclectic headteachers who paid only limited attention to the tenets of therapeutic community-style approaches that were for so long dominant in some schools of this kind. They thought it important to listen and talk to children and that addressing affective needs was similarly important but within the framework of providing an education that approximated that of a mainstream school. Similarly, they thought it was important to talk to and listen to children but not to embark on lengthy intrapsychic journeys or formal counselling. Two of the 'visited' schools were 'recovering' schools; at these a highly 'therapeutic' approach was reported to have resulted in low educational standards where 'acting out,' albeit possibly legitimate and even desirable, had degenerated into 'out-of-control'. At one of these, the new headteacher had instigated a regime based on close supervision, a carefully planned physical environment and a positive reinforcement points system. His belief was that most children deemed EBD could 'forget how to misbehave' and thereby experience the ego-boosting experience of behaving like 'normal' children; this, he believed, was genuine therapy:

'These are ordinary kids. We must believe they can achieve normal things . . . they are never as bad as their records suggest.' [M103]

Another headteacher regretted that a small minority of his pupils could not be financed to attend specialist therapeutic communities but advocated firm boundary setting and a more behaviourist approach for the majority of his pupils.

The belief in the benefit of the tightly structured yet caring establishment where children are viewed as 'normal', even when it is well understood that they experience much inner emotional turmoil, is developed in an OFSTED report on a caring school with a points system and a SMT with a traditional, directive style. All the pupils, dressed in uniform, were observed by the authors, to stand up in silence as the headteacher entered to preside over a formal morning assembly. Imposed order was transposed in the inspector's view into: 'The school's success in enabling pupils to gain control over their behaviour'. The achievement of this good order then 'has a positive effect on the quality of learning'. This philosophy seemed to be shared by the SMT of the schools we visited. Redl and Wineman's (1952) 'controls from within' are believed to develop more successfully where staff confidently impose controls from without.

Some decades ago, Gouldner (1956) noted the tendency of workers to be either 'local' or 'cosmopolitan' in outlook. This typification is germane to SMTs in schools for pupils with EBD. Ideally, it would appear that the senior staff should manage to be both but if not, the senior management team needs to contain representatives of both tendencies with the 'local' member/s of SMTs attending to within-school process issues while the 'cosmopolitan' member/s attend to factors which impinge on the school from the outside. The proficient school is responsive to the world at large but at the same time to the minutiae of daily living which are often of greater immediacy to the children and staff. The SMT has to be cognisant of the law and national demands and standards of accountability whilst simultaneously aware of Millham *et al.*'s (1975) finding that in residential establishments – we would argue similarly for day schools for children with EBD – that crises often erupt over small matters such as lunch being served late, the heating not working, or minor school procedures not being followed rather than over a school's performance against national criteria.

It is likely to be an ongoing task for SMT to respond to 'local' and 'cosmopolitan' tendencies amongst staff. Some staff can be prevented by the daily demands placed upon them from seeing the, sometimes overriding, importance of the bigger picture. For instance, the demands of the OFSTED inspection process may seem irrelevant to staff until they are actually subject to an inspection, or the 1989 Children Act guidance may be ignored until the suspension of a colleague after an allegation of abuse. On the other hand, the 'cosmopolitan' must be helped to appreciate the wisdom of Ward's (1980) assertion (supporting that of Millham *et al.* referred to above) that it is how the little things of daily life are handled in school which determine quality and client response.

Management and policy documentation

The nature of a school's leadership can also be seen in the scope and quality of a school's documentation and the processes which go into compiling and updating it. Though it is a time-consuming chore, the compilation of comprehensive documentation covering all aspects of a school's operations seems crucially important to effectiveness. The evidence from OFSTED inspections and those of HMI in the 1970s and 1980s indicates that schools with good paperwork are more likely to be effective organisations than those without. Our use of 'good' here assumes that these will be working documents, not gathering dust on top shelves or wedging open doors. As McMaster (1982) advised, theory should direct practice but practice must also correct theory; the two should be in constant dialogue. Policy documentation is a school's necessary theory. In many of the 'good practice' schools the contents of policy documents were familiar to staff who felt that they had contributed to discussions and reviews of policies resulting in a sense of ownership which aided their implementation and subsequent development. Staff responded positively to attractively presented and jargon-free documentation as a source of 'refresher' training, as induction material for new staff and as a practical guide to action in unusual circumstances. Documentation is also a public yardstick against which the school is measured by inspectors – does the school practise what it preaches?

A wide range of documentation, including prospectuses, school development plans, post-inspection action plans, behaviour management policies, health and safety documents, timetables and miscellaneous components of school handbooks has been examined by the authors. We are left agreeing with OFSTED that clear and comprehensive documentation seems to aid good practice and subscribe to the view that the processes which are gone through in developing documents are as important as the end product. These documents show that schools have clearly thought deeply about three basic questions:

- Where are we as a school?
- Where are we trying to get to?
- How are we going to get there?

In good schools the documentation is constructed and updated and amended as part of a 'do–review–learn–apply' cycle. But Millham *et al.* (1975) warn of the 'comfort of the familiar' and in inward-looking institutions, established practice, even when reviewed, can remain poor practice. As part of the evaluation process it is necessary to step back on a regular basis and to think again on the fundamental questions 'Why does the school exist?' and 'What are its aims?' before focusing on existing systems and practice which might be contrary to its 'mission'. If wide discrepancies exist between theory and practice, then medium-term aims and short-term objectives and the methods of reaching these need adjusting.

Behaviour management policies

The management of difficult or unusual behaviour and the development of a child's social and emotional well-being, following Laslett (1977), is still seen by virtually every school as the primary reason for their existence. Education, including many aspects of the National Curriculum delivered through a mainstream-style timetable, is believed to be very important but ultimately is secondary to personal and social development. By way of example, one school's preface to its behaviour management policy entitled 'The Purpose of xxx School' states that:

'xxx' provides a more appropriate setting and management for pupils with EBD who have found mainstream school unsuccessful at present. 'xxx' aims to provide a safe, secure and stimulating educational environment which responds to individual pupil's needs, where pupils may:

- regain self-esteem

- increase confidence

- become re-motivated and gain a sense of purpose in learning

- experience progress, achievement and success

- develop emotional maturity and stability

- develop positive inter-personal and social skills

- acquire life-skills which enable them to make their own sound choices

- learn to function independently

- make progress towards successful re-integration to mainstream school. [M035]

Only on the second page entitled 'The principles upon which the work of the school is based' is the standard statement that 'Each pupil is entitled to a balanced and broadly based curriculum which includes the National Curriculum and RE'.

As a second example, a 'visited' school described its mission as being:

To provide our pupils with a greater insight into their behaviour, improve their self-esteem via educational success; gain respect for themselves and others and ultimately to return to mainstream education.

Soon afterwards appears the phrase: 'Our aim is to maximise academic and social abilities in equal measure.' The educational task is described in detail later but these two examples are typical of the priorities on which schools for pupils with EBD, including those praised by OFSTED, base their educational arrangements. At a school with a strong mainstream orientation, with well-resourced classrooms, good teaching and an emphasis on the National Curriculum, the headteacher said with some feeling that: 'It's more to do with working with a desperately hurt child – with helping that child come to terms with his difficulties.' Behaviour management and assisting pupils' social development are schools' area of expertise, their distinguishing feature, their reason for existence alongside the important need to provide a challenging and appropriate education.

Management and school development plans

If a school did not appreciate the importance attached by OFSTED to school development plans before its inspection it would subsequently, as these are stressed in inspectors' reports. Good practice does exist in many schools where daily pressures contribute to a lack of formal strategic planning. However, the commitment of staff to implementing these plans is more likely to be achieved if they have been recorded in some detail on paper, having been produced with the involvement of as many of the staff as possible.

Both behaviour and education as well as other aspects of school life figure prominently in the effective school's development plan. This is an important management tool, assisting clarity of thinking in relation to the direction of the school, the way in which pupil and staff needs are being met and the points at which progress in these areas will be evaluated.

Some headteachers, LEA officers and independent school proprietors may curse the SDP as a hostage to fortune which can too easily haunt them or be used as an offensive weapon by inspectors and staff; but in the main the value of the SDP is clearly recognised as the returns to our survey show. Virtually every school claimed to have one and close to 16 per cent of respondents said it had a 'profound' influence on their school's development; 49 per cent 'much'; 30 per cent 'some' and only 5 per cent 'very little'.

The key to ensuring that plans are maximally useful and effective would seem to be for ambitions for the school to be realistic and realisable – although OFSTED may press for an uncomfortably rapid rate of change and may at times seem oblivious to the myriad of constraints imposed by human, financial and physical resource issues. Our study suggests two basic principles to follow. First the SDP should grow naturally from an ongoing audit of the schools' mission and present functioning. Secondly, it must be 'owned' certainly by a school's key players but ideally by all the school staff. The literature on effective schools (e.g. Reynolds and Cuttance 1992) indicates that if staff feel part of the review and target-setting process in relation to curriculum and resource allocation they are likely to be more committed to the desired goals. So a key issue is how this ownership can be fostered.

Good SDPs have a clear logical structure. Commonly there is a potted version of the school's mission statement as a preface while the main body will contain sections covering all areas of school life:

- plans for development of human resources on and off site (development of staffing structures, balance and individual support and INSET; links with external professionals and families);
- plans for improvements to education and care provision to better address individual and group pupil needs;
- rolling programme for physical resources including educational and care equipment, support items such as minibuses, buildings and furnishings, improvement of external site.

Running through the SDP sections will be guidance on prioritisation and financial resource allocation.

The physical presentation of SDPs varies. Some are written in dense continuous prose, while others are produced on clever computer-generated forms which do not always seem particularly suited to the content and obstruct as much as aid communication; perhaps the most user-friendly which we saw were multi-columned 'landscape' forms (i.e. A4 sheets used on their side). Whatever the design, each sheet in the better SDPs allowed for reference to all areas of a school's operation; aims; objectives; methods; persons responsible; evaluation criteria; resource implications and monitoring or completion schedule. In future some schools' SDPs are likely to be synonymous with their post-OFSTED action plan; certainly the requirement to produce the latter is likely to re-shape a school's SDP, often necessitating a major review.

The response of senior management to recent legislation

Recent legislation has brought changes to resource management and evaluation and accountability. Of particular note also in relation to pupils with EBD has been the impact of the 1989 Children Act.

Local Management of Special Schools (LMSS)

Despite the extra work it has involved, many respondents to our survey have found local management of schools a liberating experience. Of 108 schools answering this question, 44 per cent said they had a 'very positive' opinion of LMSS; 42 per cent a 'favourable' opinion; 9 per cent were 'accepting but cool'; and 5 per cent 'negative'. When asked how they coped with it, 29 per cent said 'easily'; 41 per cent 'fairly easily'; 25 per cent 'with some difficulty'; and only 5 per cent 'with much difficulty'. Comments made in interview revealed that some headteachers enjoyed the freedom it gave; it facilitated implementation of SDP priorities and enabled them to proceed with ideas at which LEAs may have balked. The majority welcomed the flexibility given by controlling their own budgets but a number said they were grateful that they had a secretary, or bursar, to operate the financial control programmes.

OFSTED inspections

The legal framework governing OFSTED inspections is provided by Section 9 of the Education (Schools) Act 1992. In contrast to many schools' view of their mission (as exemplified in the previous section), the focus of the framework is on what is offered during the hours of classroom instruction and the delivery of the National Curriculum. The inspectors have a statutory duty to report upon:

- the quality of education provided by the school;
- the educational standards achieved in the school;
- whether the financial resources made available to the school are managed efficiently;
- the spiritual, moral, social and cultural development of pupils at the school. (OFSTED 1995d, p. 8)

In Part A of the subsequent OFSTED guidance, the order of the four strands is then altered with 'Educational Standards' placed before 'Quality of Education' which subsumes 'Spiritual, moral, social and cultural development' (SMSCD). Part B is devoted to assessment of National Curriculum subject delivery. 'Attitudes, behaviour and personal development' is a sub-section of 'Educational Standards' while 'Support, guidance and pupils' welfare' follows SMSCD under 'Quality of Education'. Comments on what most headteachers see as the major reason for their schools' existence must therefore be squeezed into three, usually very brief sub-sections of inspection reports.

Although the 1995 revision of the inspection process made concessions to special schools by allowing inspectors to make judgements on pupil progress against initial baselines rather than in comparison to standards obtaining in mainstream schools, the model remains a mainstream one prompting the comment from one respondent, whose school was inspected in February 1996:

> 'Painful! Very stressful. Little relation to the primary EBD needs of the pupils. Why is the same framework used for an inner city EBD school as for a suburbs' Comp sending pupils to Oxbridge?' [M076]

This reflected other comments in similar vein. A document produced as a cathartic exercise by the staff of a school which fared relatively well in its report asserted that: 'A system which judges special schools according to the same criteria as mainstream schools is denying the need for special education.' This staff claimed that helping children to become receptive to education and to learn social skills 'that will enable individuals to function successfully in society' were fundamental elements of their work, 'yet there appears to be no facility within the reporting of the inspection process, to recognise and celebrate the achievements made within such areas.' Another respondent wrote succinctly:

> 'Too much emphasis on curriculum and not enough on EBD.' [M132]

Comments were made along similar lines and also about the imbalance and blinkered nature of the OFSTED model during school visits. In the light of comments made in Chapter 4, it is not surprising that headteachers could not understand how the contributions of care and support staff, who worked every bit as hard as the teachers ahead of and during the inspection week, were generally ignored by inspectors during their visits and in written reports. While teachers received plaudits, the role of other staff in promoting personal and social development and meeting affective needs were passed over. One senior manager claimed it took many months of hard work to rebuild morale in the aftermath of the publication of their report which had fostered divisions between teachers and other workers.

Suspicions about the quality of some members of inspection teams also surfaced in our survey returns. For two schools the process had been:

> 'Difficult – not helped by me being a Registered Inspector. Team lacked EBD experience – four out of six had been admin/advisors for 20 years. One had been headteacher of an "M" school.' [M124]

> 'Appalling, inaccurate and very, very destructive. Set us back two years at least. A whole team of apprentice inspectors – only one registered. Minimum notice and inspected during the last week of term – children terrified of going home.' [M189]

However, in two 'good practice' schools whose inspections had been led by the same Registered Inspector, one headteacher berated her while the other praised her fairness and said it was a helpful experience. Importantly many favourable responses were also received:

'Excellent – very constructive, positive report.' [N01]

'A lot of hard work and stress in preparation. The actual week was a positive experience.' [N04]

'Useful external audit.' [M129]

The headteacher of a school which received many OFSTED plaudits described the process as:

'Positive – identified strengths and confirmed those areas the school was working on' but 'Expensive – what could I have done with the money spent on the inspection!' [M108]

This was not the only comment which questioned 'value for money'. Do the complexities of the present system actually elicit a fuller, or fairer, picture of quality than the work of HMI pre-OFSTED?

Given the comments on the work and stress involved, inspectors not understanding the difficulties of working with EBD and general complaints about the model, it was surprising that so many respondents agreed that the process had aided their school's development – the intention described in the OFSTED guidance. Of 71 respondents whose schools had been inspected, almost 35 per cent said that it had aided their school 'substantially'; 34 per cent 'to some extent'; 18 per cent 'little'; and just under 13 per cent 'not at all'. It should be pointed out that some opting for the last category worked in schools about to close.

Perhaps when the second round of inspection starts in schools for pupils with EBD, senior managers will be better attuned to what is expected of them and will find OFSTED's public searchlight less stressful and fairer. Given the casualties of the first round, in many schools there will be new leaders who *have* digested the implications of the legal framework under which the inspectors have to act and will have had three or four years in which to sharpen up their interpretations of the National Curriculum. But will the perceived deterioration in behaviour and increased complexity of pupil needs reported in Chapter 3 make it even more difficult for schools to perform adequately according to the OFSTED model, and can we be certain that the model will remain in its present form when the government has completed its deliberations on provision for children with EBD?

The 1989 Children Act

Recently some staff in schools for children with EBD have been found guilty of physical abuse, sexual abuse and other paedophile offences. Returns from 130 schools to our supplementary questionnaire on abuse and reactions to the 1989 Children Act indicate that between 1991 and 1996 at least 22 staff were dismissed for such abuse: five for sexual offences (one said to be 'only verbal'); 16 for physical; and one for emotional. This might be an underestimate, given that some respondents may not have been candid when completing questionnaires but clearly abuse has taken place and senior staff are very aware of the need for vigilance. Some still bear the scars of guilt for having trusted or appointed the teachers and care workers involved but clearly the abuser can 'take in' the most 'street-wise' of headteachers.

Our data also indicate that between 1991 and 1996 there were over 400 allegations of abuse against staff which led to the involvement of outside agencies, about 85 per cent of which were in residential schools. Over 90 per cent of these involved physical abuse and 5 per cent sexual but it should be noted that 6 per cent of the schools in our sample reported 41 per cent of the physical abuse allegations while 27 per cent of schools reported no allegations of physical abuse. When the number of dismissals or resignations is set against the number of allegations, about one in 20 of those accused were found guilty of serious malpractice. Responses further reveal that 74 per cent of the allegations led to 'no criticism' from the external agencies, 14 per cent to 'minor criticism' and 12 per cent to 'very minor criticism'. Seventy staff in 11 schools were reported to have been suspended, 56 took 'sick leave' and ten opted for early retirement under the pressures of investigation after false allegations. Here, of course, a dilemma is posed both for child protection workers and senior staff in schools. How can the one in 20 who is guilty be speedily weeded out and the damage done to the 19 innocents be minimised?

Some 42 per cent of schools passed a 'favourable' or 'quite favourable' judgement on the operation of their local child protection procedures; close to 30 per cent of respondents offered 'neutral' or a mixture of good and bad comment and 28 per cent 'quite negative' or 'negative'. An improving situation was reported in 8 per cent of schools usually with quicker procedures and a greater degree of understanding and empathy developing between schools and protection workers. However, the same percentage thought the procedures were damaging to staff and 7 per cent that they were unjust. The greatest injustice was seen to occur when staff are suspended without knowing of what they are accused and are thus denied the chance to defend themselves. Headteachers also considered it unfortunate that they could no longer use their knowledge, expertise and relationship with pupils and families to investigate situations immediately if they themselves were not implicated in the allegations. Prior to 1991 allegations could often be resolved in hours while enquiries by social services and police are invariably more protracted, sometimes dragging on for months and even years, causing stress for staff and disrupting the life of the school. In a few cases, an allegation has caused the unwarranted closure of a school and threatened the survival of others.

The quotations below on the child protection procedures represent the range of views expressed to us.

'Necessary, but unhappy regarding potential for false accusations.' [M019]

'The process was very long and drawn out over comparatively minor and unfounded allegations. Throughout this time the teacher is under increased stress.' [M021]

'Since 1992/3 the LEA doesn't automatically suspend staff, which can be a horrendous ordeal whether innocent or not. In the initial stages, innocent staff may feel too much belief is placed in child by social services.' [M090]

'Improved application of procedures to the benefit of staff and students. There is now a far greater knowledge and trust within the profession involved.' [M091]

'They work very well. ESW and SS cooperate well.' [M014]

'Given the number of people involved, they work remarkably smoothly.' [M087]

'Robust management/mismanagement should be dealt with separately to "child abuse" '. [R18]

To develop this last suggestion a further question must be raised – what constitutes abuse? What does the phrase 'significant harm' as employed in Section 31 of the Act (Home Office/DoH/DES 1991) mean? For example, an uncritical reading of Grimshaw with Berridge (1994) could lead to the conclusion that child abuse is prevalent in some residential schools. However, this aspect of their study, like many media reports, rests on somewhat uncertain evidence. It reports staff perceptions on the events of the previous year and lumps together reports of suspected and actual abuse. It does not say who is abusing whom or whether this took place at the school or at home. It also fails to distinguish between the different degrees and forms of physical contact which might be construed as abuse. More broadly, what to many parents, and many professionals acting in *loco parentis*, might seem a sensible, time-honoured practice, namely the slap, has been elevated into abuse which can lead to instant dismissal for staff and might soon be a crime for British parents. It is worth recalling that Wilson and Evans (1980) were 'not unduly disturbed' to find staff admitting to using occasional 'light slapping' which

> if rare and under control, can be a quick and effective way of showing disapproval to the offending child and others and as a rule the physical pain is less important than the message it conveys. (p. 164)

That short time ago, many teachers in Scottish and northern mainstream (and some special schools) walked around with leather tawses in their pockets with David Wills' (1971) injunctions on the futility and dangers of punishment having a somewhat limited impact. Practice has moved swiftly since that time but many practitioners believe that the pendulum has swung too far. The fact that physically moving a child, who is, for example, creating havoc or making learning impossible for other children, out of a room against his or her will may expose them to charges of assault clearly makes their job more difficult. Indeed, Chaplain and Freeman (1994), in their study of children's homes, claimed that the Children Act made the operation of some establishments 'almost farcical' (p. 150). 'What would society think of a parent who let their child wander off in the middle of the night?', they asked. Yet the advice given in Children Act guidance for residential care is that

> physical restraint should be used rarely and only to prevent a child harming himself or others or from damaging property. Force should not be used for any other purpose, nor simply to secure compliance with staff instructions. (Department of Health 1991a, para.1.83, p. 15)

Interestingly, our respondents were even-handed about the guidance which followed the Children Act. They recognised that it contained much sound advice, that it correctly stressed the rights of children and tried to promote the achievement of safe environments. They applauded that the child's voice should be heard. They accepted the need for social service inspection procedures and agreed that the Act contributed to better practice in many ways. However, many expressed doubts about the balance between children's rights and responsibilities. They feared the 'voice of the child' might drown out that of front-line staff. One respondent noted laconically that the Children Act 'assumes reasonableness and cooperation. These are not qualities that stand out in our pupils generally' [R19]. Another headteacher echoed this sentiment in arguing that 'there is a general assumption of objectivity and maturity on the part of the child which is ill-founded' [M052]. Yet another commented that 'Staff are in constant fear of litigation as there is too much emphasis given to the child's version of events. Members of staff are suspended on very spurious grounds' [M105].

When asked more specifically for comments on the Department of Health's guidance on physical restraint (Department of Health 1991a, b) responses were varied. Of the 112 answers 40 per cent gave a clearly negative response, complaining about vagueness; 20 per cent a favourable or satisfactory verdict; 35 per cent a neutral verdict; while 5 per cent (usually day school respondents) claimed not to be aware of their existence. The following quotations illustrate the range.

'Useless. An attempt by civil servants to cover up what they are now realising was a foolish blunder with far reaching consequences.' [M196]

'Too vague generally. The guidelines as to when it can be used appropriately need stating more clearly as does the principle of adult responsibility for control.' [A11]

'Unclear and not validated. Urgent need for specified training programme in restraint techniques with validation.' [M03]

'Clear on procedure, weak on practical applications and methods.' [M150]

'Not clear enough, still fudges the issues of restraint in cases of preventing younger children from absconding and permissible techniques.' [M122]

'Useful in formulation of our own policy.' [M073]

'Policy useful – however, there is no substitute for experience or practical advice and our LEA does not endorse any policy.' [M131]

'Very good!' [M097]

Issues relating to allegations of abuse and to physical restraint clearly pose serious dilemmas for schools and this issue remains unresolved despite helpful advice recently from the DfEE following the 1997 Education Act regarding the ability of *teachers* to restrain and remove troublesome children from class. For care staff the Department of Health (1996) has also issued a series of videos on defusing tensions and on limited restraint techniques. However, these were described as inadequate by headteachers of the 'good practice' schools we have visited, some of whom expressed preferences for commercial American packages such as 'Therapeutic Crisis Intervention' (TCI) or 'Strategies for Crisis Intervention and Prevention' (SCIP). Allen (1998) stresses that physical restraint must be viewed as a part of a wider behaviour management policy emphasising defusion and anger management and use of touch while also highlighting the dangers of certain restraint techniques and suggesting safer alternatives.

Current advice is that 'restraint' should be confined to holding a child in one place (Department of Health 1991a) and movement from that place should only be aided by 'leading by the arm'. In practice, as Laslett (1977) amongst others emphasised, there are occasions when it seems appropriate and necessary to physically move children with EBD against their wishes for the sake of other children but this requires the use of force which amounts to more than merely leading by the arm. We observed one headteacher who had turned a chaotic and out-of-control school into a very happy and relaxed community, marching a teenage pupil away from the classrooms by the application of superior force. Had the headteacher abided by DoH advice, it is highly unlikely that his intervention would have been effective and would, in all likelihood, led to ridicule from the child involved and by onlooking children with the result that general school discipline would have been undermined. There is evidence to suggest that children want firm, fair staff (Millham *et al.* 1975, Chaplain and Freeman 1994, Sanders and Hendry 1997) who can control them – or at least their peers when they are 'playing up' and inflicting misery all around. Furthermore, it is arguable that the need for physical restraint becomes a much rarer event when pupils are shown that firm action, which *in extremis* can involve physical restraint, will be taken and that senior managers will ensure that the school's policies and management strategies prevail.

One headteacher remarked, that 'looked after' children, described as out-of-control and causing serious management problems elsewhere, often settle and thrive in residential schools where staff are willing to use a more determined approach and this comment was echoed by senior staff in about half the schools we visited. But another headteacher clearly felt that the Children Act made the development and implementation of such an approach difficult:

'I struggle to find a positive response. The balance of the Act has not worked in children's favour. Falsely empowering children and at the same time shattering the confidence of those working with them is a step which will give rise to a long bitter harvest.' [M153]

There are wider issues than just physical restraint involved. Chaplain and Freeman (1994) considered that children in some residential homes were being damaged and subjected to bullying and extortion by peers, with staff feeling powerless to act because of the ramifications of the Children Act. They describe a general loss of control in some of these homes due to the emphasis on children's rights. They also report an erosion of routines and discipline to the extent that children could not be forced to wash themselves, or even change their socks. This research perhaps explains some of the difficulties the headteachers of our sample schools noted with 'looked after' children. Of course, the family difficulties and emotional disturbance of these young people could be severe but achieving 'settledness' (to use Beedell's, 1993, term) in school is not helped when pupils experienced excessively lenient approaches elsewhere.

Working with parents

Part of the task for senior management in any school is to create effective systems for obtaining and maintaining the support of their pupils' parents. As indicated in Chapter 3, parents can be suspicious of authority figures and have had their faith in teachers dented by virtue of their own prior experience. The advice of The Warnock Report (DES 1978a) and more recently DfE guidance (DfE 1994b), was that senior staff should adopt a proactive stance to win over and develop mutually helpful relationships with parents. However, a number of senior staff in our schools viewed it as beyond their task to visit students' homes: the parents should and generally did, it was claimed, attend meetings at the school when asked. At least one deputy headteacher reported that it was dangerous to be in a student's house because the parent may make allegations. However, many more schools, agreeing with Galloway (1990), apparently thought that the risk was worth taking and set great store by home visiting. It was commonly suggested in interviews with headteachers that the support of parents had to be won if there was to be a realistic chance of pupils settling in special schools; indeed lack of parental support was cited as a valid reason for refusing entry to a child. In some schools the headteacher or another senior staff member visits the child's home before the child attends a pre-admission interview at the school. Some respondents were of the opinion that it was better to talk in the less threatening environment of the parental home, over a cup of tea, than to communicate formally by letter – at least in the early stages until a trusting relationship had been established. Sadly, it was claimed that an aim of such visits might be to establish that the school staff were not like social service employees; nor, as one headteacher of a non-maintained school claimed was necessary, that they were like some 'desk-bound' mainstream SMT 'who did not want to get their hands dirty'.

At other schools the home visits only began after a child had started at the school but then continued throughout the child's placement and involved any member of staff. Different systems were apparent. Some had tried a designated social worker or home–school liaison worker but had subsequently dispensed with this, preferring to share visiting duties between SMT, middle managers and other staff. Sometimes it was the child's keyworker or class tutor who had special responsibilities. In some schools a regular pattern of monthly or termly visits was timetabled; in others it was said to happen according to need.

More frequent than home visits was communication, both planned and ad hoc, by telephone. Some respondents reported regular, sometimes daily, conversations to discuss good and bad behaviour, to plan for weekends and to maintain and develop relationships. There was also regular written contact; reference being made particularly to 'good' letters praising the achievements of the child. Examples were seen of home–school notebooks, often part of structured behaviour management schemes, which were aimed to keep the parent informed of their child's progress. Hearing positive reports was reported as often a novel experience for parents and was claimed to aid the development of supportive relationships and provide a reservoir of understanding and support for the staff when bad behaviour requiring parental support had to be confronted.

Importance was also attached by some to annual reviews and informal meetings and gatherings at the school. Some schools provide taxis or send staff to bring parents to review meetings. One headteacher told how he 'bribed' parents to attend parents' evenings by offering wine and finger buffets. A welcoming, open-door policy where headteachers see parents who arrived 'on spec' was reported by some schools as paying long-term dividends. Some schools make a point of allowing parents to sit in class or mingle with the school as it goes about its daily routine in order to instil confidence – not always popular with 'local' staff but beneficial overall, particularly where parents may be dubious about their child's placement. In a few residential schools accommodation where families can stay overnight is provided.

Overall, it was felt that parents had to be offered the opportunity of positive involvement in their child's education, which contrasted with the way they had frequently been received by their child's previous schools' staff or treated by representatives of other professions. Once a relationship and trust was established it was felt that then 'home truths' could be exchanged and deep-seated problems tackled, although SMTs were wary of getting out of their depth. It is also a task for management to see that junior staff, perhaps underrating the pitfalls, do not indulge in well-intentioned but potentially harmful interventions with parents and the advice offered by Cunningham and Davis (1985) on approaches to working with parents is relevant here. One headteacher noted that he did not see himself as a social worker but lived locally and said he sometimes met parents informally in the pub or shopping arcade. This he saw as a help in building rapport. Formal family therapy (see for example, Asen 1996) sadly seems to remain the domain of isolated health services and social service projects. Perhaps the nearest approach to this offered by a few schools were parent support groups.

Despite constraints imposed by resources and policy decisions, the work with parents undertaken by proficient EBD schools was seen to contribute to pupils' changed behaviour and emotional development. Echoing the findings of OFSTED parent questionnaires and earlier research (e.g. ILEA 1985) a majority of parents are reported as being positive towards the school and their child's placement there. The cynic might say that this is because the children, especially those in residential schools, are 'out of their hair' and consequently stresses within the home are lessened but we heard more frequently that the parents were happy because for the first time in many years their children were settled, doing well and receiving good reports. Grimshaw (1995) similarly found that 85 per cent of the parents had 'a good opinion' of four residential EBD schools attended by their children while one OFSTED report contained the comment:

> Parents perceive the school to be very successful at managing behaviour and are supportive of the work the school does.

Also to be remembered are the findings of Wilson and Evans (1980), Cooper (1993), Howe (1995) and Sanders and Hendry (1997) who note pupil appreciation of many aspects of their placements in special schools; pupils speaking to the present research team added further similar evidence.

It was therefore not surprising that respondents to our survey reported a generally positive parental reaction to their child's placement at the sample schools. Fifty per cent were said to be 'very positive' with a further 30 per cent 'favourable', 14 per cent 'accepting but cool' and 6 per cent 'negative' with a slightly greater degree of satisfaction claimed for residential schools. These are, of course, the views of headteachers rather than those of the parents themselves and must therefore be treated with caution even though they do accord with evidence from other sources.

Staff management

A fundamental task for senior staff is choosing the right staff and subsequently supporting their development. Stoll and Fink (1994) noted that 'the key to improved student learning is enhanced teacher learning' (p. 159) and the same can be said for care and support staff. Developing and caring for staff should commence before the first day of their formal employment and continue throughout their time in post; it is too easy to overlook chinks which appear in the confident facade of competent long-serving staff. Handy (1976) in discussing the motivation of workers referred to their 'E' factor – their willingness to put their energy, enthusiasm and time into their work. How can a school harness and then sustain the E factor of staff over years to develop and maintain their proficiency in school?

Selection

OFSTED expects high standards of subject expertise and yet in some areas of the country it is very difficult to recruit teachers, especially in music and foreign languages. The image of the EBD school was also held up by respondents as a problem in recruitment. The headteacher of one school noted that many mainstream colleagues she knew would make superb teachers of pupils with EBD and would enjoy it – if only they could be persuaded to enter a world they perceived as alien. Another headteacher said how important he thought it was for him to wear a smart suit when attending gatherings of teachers where he made a point of not talking about 'awful children'; he chose instead to report his pupils' GCSE successes to counteract mainstream perceptions of his teachers as well as his pupils. The unfortunate publicity generated by child abuse scandals and poor OFSTED reports has not assisted the image of the EBD school. Consequently, national and local advertising can produce disappointing results – unless, of course, the school is close to the Lake District and an outdoor pursuits specialist is wanted.

For the above reasons, headteachers often resort to head-hunting through whatever networks they enjoy, mixed with a policy of promotion from existing staff. Sometimes, impressive supply teachers or part-time staff are offered permanent full-time positions. If outside appointments do have to be made, then as indicated in Chapter 4, personal characteristics take precedence over subject expertise, although it is hoped that both can be present in candidates. A choice might also have to be made between hiring keen and hopefully malleable young staff or experienced teachers who might be set in the contrasting traditions of other schools. We heard more than one headteacher complain that experienced and senior teachers transferring from other EBD schools and arriving with glowing references had not lived up to expectations and were now serious obstacles in the path of the school's development, adding to pressures on the headteacher – particularly if they had been appointed to the senior management team. On the other hand, one headteacher, trying to restore the fortunes of a school placed in special measures when under different management, was emphatic that he needed teachers with EBD experience, who were good at relationships, understood behaviour and could restore order in the classrooms where a succession of subject specialists had failed.

We also heard arguments in favour of primary-trained staff because they were said to be more accustomed to group work, flexible teaching demands and could tune in more easily to the academic levels of pupils who had fallen behind in the basic subjects. Against this, some headteachers, responding to OFSTED concerns about National Curriculum delivery, or believing that the discipline of teachers used to working with Years 9, 10 and 11 might be stronger, were searching for experienced secondary-trained teachers.

A complex picture emerges from the data. However, if schools appoint using the traditional practice of interviewing from a short-list gathered through advertising, best practice appears to suggest that spreading interviews over two days, in which candidates are seen in a range of situations and staff and pupils have an opportunity to provide feedback to the interview panel can enhance the likelihood of good appointments. Observing candidates in their existing place of work to gain a feel for the ethos from which they are coming and a glimpse of their operating style also seems to constitute increasingly common practice. Unfortunately appointments sometimes have to be made in a hurry. Feedback and experience suggest that this can all too often be a case of 'act in haste, repent at leisure'. In this circumstance short-term appointments or 'trial periods' provide possible safeguards against poor appointments.

Short-term appointments may also be applicable to the appointment of RSWs where, as has been mentioned, the pool of experienced staff is limited but 'grow-your-own' policies seem common (Jacka 1960) in relation to residential care. We saw in our visits, for example, dinner ladies who had become classroom assistants and cooks who had become care workers. We are mindful of Millham *et al.*'s (1975) view that qualifications do not necessarily equal better practice in this field, particularly in the absence (see Chapter 4) of respected and accepted accredited training. If outside appointments are made, common practice appears to be to offer them on a trial basis with a probationary period before making a permanent offer.

Induction

For some new staff initial experiences in a school for EBD children can be more problematic than anticipated. 'It's not nice', a deputy headteacher remarked to us, 'when they swear at you. You have to realise that it's not personal.' But that advice may take time to sink in. Another respondent described the different qualities required of special school compared to mainstream staff: 'An ability to remain calm, positive and humorous when under extreme provocation and being attacked by weapons and missiles' [M204]. New staff need support – and not just on the first day of term.

A KS4 coordinator noted how on her transfer from a mainstream school the children 'gave her hell' for her first term. She was finding the process of adjustment difficult; her pupils knew it and did not expect her to stay. It was only after the first holidays, when to their surprise, she returned to school, that they realised she meant business. It was only then that they began to form relationships with her and her job became easier. Was it necessary for this to happen in this way? In one school we visited an attempt was made to alleviate the problem by allocating each new teacher a senior mentor who is timetabled to watch colleagues in action, to team-teach and allow the teacher to gradually take on his or her full duties; in short to learn the ropes and to see the pupils' expectations of staff before taking on full responsibility. A similar sort of induction training might be even more important for RSWs, who commonly start with no previous experience of working with difficult youngsters.

There are confident staff who prefer to establish themselves and have the ability to do this from the outset. They still need watching but this can be done from a distance, with tactical interventions made discreetly. All new members of staff need some guidance to avoid early mistakes.

The monitoring and development of performance

The positive response to supervision for RSWs which was outlined in the previous chapter suggests that this could be used as a vehicle for professional development as well as a means of personal support. An extension of this system might also be of benefit to other employees, including teachers. A number of our schools reported that they have staff support group meetings in addition to normal 'business' staff meetings. Some blend the two, using after-duty debriefings as an opportunity to discuss how situations were handled and how they might have been approached to better effect.

The lack of external training has been covered in the previous chapter and will not be addressed here other than to wonder how some schools manage to send staff on courses and perceive these as useful while others find it difficult and seem to think it of limited use. Is it all a question of finances and resources or might some schools be suffering because management adopts an inward-looking perspective? Some respondents alluded to links with neighbourhood schools as providing a practical and immediately useful form of training with special and mainstream teachers observing and sharing practice, seeing alternative materials being used and learning from each other. References were also made to LEA advisory input and INSET, with value attached to assistance given with National Curriculum issues. The local educational psychologist visited one 'good practice' school for a half day a fortnight, devoting some of this time to developing care staff's counselling skills and assisting them with individual care planning.

Nearly every school claimed to run an appraisal system. However, for many schools this seemed to be a somewhat perfunctory process, with employees only being appraised once a year and sometimes, once in two or even three years. However, 41 per cent of 135 respondents claimed that it aided teachers' professional development either 'very significantly' or 'significantly' and 50 per cent said 'a little', leaving 9 per cent saying that it did not. Whether this is a useful approach would seem to depend on the seriousness with which it is taken. It seems likely that in some schools there are well-established and regular systems with target setting and regular monitoring, with teachers and management making commitments to each other. In such schools teachers and senior management believe the processes are beneficial and ego-boosting, with praise and encouragement as well as suggestions for improved performance. If teachers fail to praise children sufficiently (Merrett 1993) sometimes senior staff are also wanting in 'catching staff being good'. Respondents were further asked whether appraisal systems helped management achieve its goals; similar percentages were found with nearly 42 per cent saying 'very significantly'(5 per cent) or 'significantly'.

When it comes to the creation of opportunities for staff to discuss their worries, to seek reassurance and sometimes emotional support, informal processes seem to be the norm. Indeed the Head of Care of one school we visited reported that he had dispensed with a formal system of supervision for care staff in favour of an 'open door' policy on the grounds that often staff would not be helped if they were told to wait for their supervision session in the following week to discuss a pressing concern. Teachers, headteachers and other senior staff generally seem to opt for an informal, open door policy. It was commonly said that support was often offered by other colleagues in the staff room or outside work: Hanko (1995) argued that teachers in EBD schools seemed more prepared to confess to difficulties and to seek solace and encouragement among colleagues than many mainstream teachers. Again, debriefings or small group staff meetings or in-house reviews might offer opportunities to talk about difficulties; to discover that others are similarly challenged by a pupil can be a reassuring experience. Occasionally, in a therapeutic community, a consultant psychotherapist, or elsewhere a student counsellor or visiting psychologist, had time set aside in which staff could seek counselling for themselves, and in one or two local authorities and independent organisations there were telephone counselling services.

Finally, as well as suggesting the need for after-school meetings, one school ventured: 'Regular supplies of beer/wine and cigarettes from France. Humour!' Once again the theme of 'laughing through common adversity' emerges as a defence and support mechanism when working with pupils with EBD.

Maintaining the E factor

The paragraphs above refer to the maintenance of staff motivation. Various management theorists have pointed out that it takes far more than reasonable salary levels and hours of work (Handy 1976) to obtain the optimum performance from employees and that the Maslow triangle applies as much to them as to children. Barriers in the way of fostering self-esteem, self-actualisation and feelings of belonging may contribute to neglect or abuse of normal physiological needs. The work is stressful (Upton 1996) and there are dangers that this is alleviated by excessive dependence on alcohol and tobacco or by staff adopting irregular eating patterns. Certainly the life-styles of some long-stay staff is a cause for concern.

In our study we gathered information on how staff relaxed. SMTs reported a range of activities including: cross-country, skiing, rock climbing, sailing, amateur dramatics, trips to London to watch Shakespeare, golf, rallying, reading, Tai Chi and serving behind the bar in a local pub on a Friday night. Some even found time for their own families. However, the general message was clear for all workers with children with EBD. Having interests – even worries – outside work does tend to preserve and extend useful working life and counter the creation of blinkered, idiosyncratic practice.

Conclusion

In this chapter we have only been able to look at some of the functions of management. No striking features relating to management responsibilities emerged on a number of routine issues including how staff should be deployed, whether they should live on or off site, what administration periods should be provided, what size groups staff should have to work with and optimal duty and teaching timetabling. These are obviously important considerations for SMTs who have to act in the light of local traditions and the art of the possible. Proficient senior staff certainly see the potential of how they arrange these matters for maintaining the freshness and general mental health of the staff while addressing the instrumental and expressive needs of the children.

Chapter 6

Addressing Pupil Needs

In the first chapter of this book we adopted Kerr's (1968) wide definition of curriculum. We were also taken by Wilson and Evan's (1980) comment that 'treatment' consists of 'whatever is provided in schools . . . to further the personal, social or educational readjustment of disturbed pupils' and that this 'cannot be restricted to curriculum content and teaching methods' (p. 28).

In this chapter we report our findings on how time is spent in class, during breaks and the evening and weekend care hours. After examining some general issues, we discuss our findings in relation to the curriculum, before focusing on the principles and systems of behaviour management. In the last section we turn to our data on break times, mealtimes and care.

Care in education–education in care

Education and care are not two discrete entities in provision for pupils with EBD. Teachers, care staff and those with pastoral responsibilities need to work together for the social and educational development of the pupils. This we found to be the case in our good practice residential schools, while in proficient day schools we also encountered staff paying close attention to the social, emotional and physical needs of pupils both in, and outside, the classroom. In our good practice day schools we discovered that some senior teaching staff had in fact previously worked in residential care posts, as had most of the teachers in a successful day school we visited, perhaps fostering their concern for the whole child. Other senior teachers undertook evening care duties and seemed to share Greenhalgh's (1994) view that 'the emotion that lies behind action' must proceed hand in hand with assisting pupils' cognitive development; or, to use the terminology of Bernstein (1977, p. 38), that pursuing goals relating to the 'instrumental order' (e.g. targets in reading ability or national accredited courses such as GCSE) will be assisted by paying careful attention to needs which relate to the 'expressive order' (conduct and 'character training'). The importance of this was confirmed by Millham *et al.* (1975) who found that for Home Office approved schools 'the schools which stress pastoral care are those that achieve effective results' (p. 122) while Galloway (1990) advanced the same message in relation to mainstream educational provision.

While style and presentation might alter according to whether a classroom or care setting is involved and the professionals who are participating, we believe that education, in its wide sense, is often provided through care; and care through good classroom teaching (Cole 1986).

Effective teachers, as Greenhalgh (1994), Galloway (1990) and Stoll and Fink (1994) stress, are concerned about the affective as well as the cognitive. Further, as Wilson and Evans (1980) emphasise, educational success can be a therapeutic experience, building pupils' self-image and confidence, helping to settle a young person's emotional turmoil and overt challenging behaviour.

Conversely, the pupils' life-space outside the classroom can be used as an educative medium as Bettelheim (1950), Redl and Wineman (1952), Trieschman *et al.* (1969), Dockar-Drysdale (1968), Lennhoff (1968) and other pioneers argued. The delivery of primary care and addressing 'belonging' and 'esteem' needs can pave the way for educational growth in the formal classroom setting.

Some writers have argued (e.g. Brennan 1985) that in residential provision education should be pursued in the evening care hours. They do not simply have in mind pupils doing homework; indeed, given the expense of residential education and the extent of the educational difficulties of the pupils involved, it would seem essential that residential schools provide more than dinner, bed and breakfast. What is needed is for care staff to adopt a 'horticultural' approach, fostering personal growth through the provision in care hours of a rich range of activities in addition to providing good quality primary care (Dockar-Drysdale 1968), and allowing for the genuine free time advocated by Beedell (1970). The commonly used term '24 hour curriculum' stresses the need to consciously use parts of the evenings and weekends to aid the social and educational development of the pupils.

In this way, RSWs might live up to the greater professionalism associated with the European concept of the 'social pedagogue' (Davies Jones 1986), being expected to provide good basic care but at the same time being a versatile 'activity person' (p. 88), trained to stimulate, engage and motivate the children. Activity is used as a bridge which links adult to young person and helps develop a therapeutic relationship.

Matching provision to the aims of education

Our data indicate that the education programmes in the schools which we surveyed fall within the wide parameters set by the long-term goals of education as defined by the Warnock Committee (DES 1978a):

> They are first, to enlarge a child's knowledge, experience and imaginative understanding, and thus his awareness of moral values and capacity for enjoyment; and secondly, to enable him to enter the world after formal education is over as an active participant in society and a responsible contributor to it, capable of achieving as much independence as possible. The educational goals of every child are determined in relation to these goals. (p. 5)

This statement stresses the need for the curriculum of schools for pupils with EBD to meet social, emotional and behavioural goals as well as more strictly educational requirements and for it to be offered both in and outside the classroom by teachers, RSWs, LSAs and other staff. Such a programme requires careful planning to address individual pupil needs in all areas and this is what we found in our 'good practice' schools. We concur with the attention paid in OFSTED reports to the importance of staff knowing where they are with a child at any time and where they are heading in the short, medium and long term. Examples of documentation were examined and in good practice schools we found well thought-out, comprehensive, yet user-friendly, systems for assessing, recording and reviewing in both instrumental and expressive domains. In line with the mainstream 'effectiveness' literature, they also engaged pupils in this process, helping to foster 'ownership' of their learning at all stages.

The concern of Warnock for the preparation of pupils for life as adults in society is of particular relevance, given the findings of Dawson (1980) that pupils on average attended schools for the 'disturbed' for about four years. The data from our research paint a similar picture. A few schools do achieve better rates of reintegration; one school claimed a 95 per cent re-inclusion rate. However, the usual pattern is that once a child has been labelled EBD and placed in segregated provision then that child will see out his or her schooldays in special schooling. Statements about reintegration contained in many schools' documentation often remain pious hopes. In interviews in the good practice schools we were repeatedly told of the resistance of mainstream schools to re-admit pupils. It was also claimed that some pupils, reflecting parental wishes, did not wish to be re-included. After many troubled years in the mainstream, the child had settled in a special school and there existed supportive relations between pupils, their families and staff which it seemed unwise to disrupt. Having felt excluded, their placement in a special school had given them that sense of belonging which Maslow (1970) indicates is of crucial importance for emotional health.

Of our sample 70 per cent were reported to have attended their special school for two or more years and about 37 per cent for three or more years. Junior schools achieved reintegration for a minority at Year 7 but hopes that early intervention might lead to re-inclusion, and less expense, at the secondary phase were not apparently being achieved. Overall, our questionnaire data suggest that, on average, less than two pupils per year per special school will transfer back to the mainstream. This finding is consistent with that of the Audit Commission (1992).

Nor was the part-time integration of pupils in local mainstream provision as envisaged by Underwood (Ministry of Education 1955) and Warnock (DES 1978a) a common practice. Where it happened it was usually KS4 pupils attending further education colleges for vocational training or occasionally a small school taking advantage of the better facilities of the local comprehensive school. In both situations, the amount of functional integration, with pupils mixing freely with the students of the host institutions, was limited.

What implications does 'once EBD/always EBD' labelling have for planning education and care? Clearly, given the need for programming to be responsive to individual need, retaining the ambition to re-include some pupils, particularly those placed in special schools in KS1 or 2 or early in KS3 should not be dropped but perhaps for older pupils it should be more overtly stated that the teenage pupil is highly likely to remain in the special school and that the second of the Warnock goals, preparation for self-supporting, independent adulthood, should be stressed. Returns from 77 schools suggest that over half of their school leavers progress to further education and a quarter into employment, leaving a quarter whose destination is unknown. Planning should also recognise that disaffection can increase with age: in the USA some 40 per cent of pupils with emotional disturbance aged 14 or over drop out (Nelson and Pearson 1991). As has long been recognised (Hargreaves 1967; DES 1989c), many 14- to 16-year-olds might benefit from more extensive provision of 'alternative' and accredited vocational courses.

'Normalisation'

Maier (1981) posits that the principle of 'normalisation' should guide the provision of residential child care. In the context of special schools for pupils with EBD, we define this concept as meaning the provision of an educational curriculum for these children which mirrors closely that provided for their peers in mainstream schools. It also means allowing pupils to see and to experience a range of 'normal' experiences in open society which mirror those experienced by children attending day schools.

As the Schools Council Project (Dawson 1980) found, and our research confirms, pupils in schools for children with EBD want to experience much the same curricula as their peers in mainstream schools. This extends to taking SATs and GCSE, or accredited vocational courses, however much difficulty this may cause for teachers in motivating the pupils to do the required work. Replies to our questionnaire and comments made by staff and pupils to the authors on their visits underline that pupils with EBD do not wish to be seen as a breed apart, unworthy of the full curriculum entitlement as mandated by law. Year 11 pupils stressed to the authors that they recognised the importance of GCSEs to their career prospects but, if they could not attain good grades in these, then other nationally recognised accreditation was valued.

The desire of pupils for 'normalisation' was clearly recognised by most SMTs in our good practice schools in planning both the education and care curricula. They appeared conscious both of the danger that pupils in special schools may be isolated in a somewhat artificial world and of the need for pupils to mix in the wider community. Most schools, particularly residential schools, claimed in their responses to actively seek means by which their pupils could experience aspects of local community life. There were references to allowing pupils out in the local village or town when their behaviour allowed this degree of trust to be accorded to them; to involvement of pupils in local youth clubs, scouts, cadets, sporting competitions and outdoor pursuit expeditions; to trips out on a regular basis for shopping, swimming, cinema, places of interest and the normal experience of 'going out', for example, to McDonalds. There were also references to community service in the form of assisting in retirement homes, or clubs for those with learning disabilities and the benefits this had in opening the eyes of young people to different facets of society.

In general there would seem to be an awareness in good practice schools that high standards of behaviour achieved within the school premises need to be tested in the greater reality of the wider world. However, some schools, usually day schools or those operating only four-day boarding, did not see this as a particularly important aspect of their care or education programmes. As one school put it:

'We are five-day boarding and we encourage many of our boarders to be part-time so they can mix more readily in their local community, not ours.' [M135]

One day school visited by the authors pointed out that, in reality, mixing in the community was often not feasible as the pupils had often been excluded from local youth clubs and the like. This headteacher was either realistic or lacked persistence in trying to alter a disappointing situation.

The importance of 'rubber boundaries'

Greenhalgh (1994), reflecting earlier child care writers such as Maier (1981), stressed that independence can only grow from healthy dependence on teachers and other care-givers. Getting pupils with EBD to this first stage of trusting and relating positively to adults can often take a very long time and is highly dependent on the existence of regular routines and structured use of class and care time.

In this context, Redl (1966) talked of the 'great ego-supportive power of traditionalised routine'. The clear message from our data, backing up that from Millham *et al.* (1975) and Wilson and Evans (1980), is that to increase the happiness of pupils with EBD, to help them feel secure and to form beneficial relationships on which greater independence can grow, they need the highly structured communities noted by OFSTED inspectors in 'good practice' schools. There has to be order and discipline with the adults clearly in charge.

The authors' data suggest little support for the view which was common in the 1950s, and which finds expression in the Underwood Report (Ministry of Education 1955), that it is sometimes healthy and necessary for the maladjusted to 'act out' their disturbance as part of the therapeutic process. Acting out clearly does happen and needs to be handled sympathetically, but it is no longer seen by most as being sensible to adopt a permissive stance. Indeed, in one school the view was expressed that pupils should be helped to 'forget how to misbehave' by being introduced and occupied with pro-social activity which they will find increasingly rewarding. Controls from without promote the 'controls from within' of which Redl and Wineman (1952) talked. Our data show a firm belief in the need for systems of rewards and sanctions linked to listening and talking to pupils. Structures, we were told should be there in class, at break times and in the care hours to aid adult control and to facilitate pupil self-control; at the same time, allowance has to be made for the undoubted emotional and behavioural turmoil present in the pupils. Systems must retain flexibility so that they can bend and adapt to individual needs; they must not hurt individual pupils whilst providing structure, routines and rules for all. One headteacher used the memorable phrase 'rubber boundaries' to describe this (Amos 1997).

From these general observations we now turn to more detailed reporting of our findings. We focus upon proficiency in schools not children's homes, so despite our concern to underline the importance of what happens at break times and in the care hours, and our belief (following e.g. Laslett 1977) that the personal and social development of pupils is a primary need, we concentrate first on our findings in relation to the education curriculum ahead of considering arrangements for outside class activities, because that is also a primary need.

Class-time provision

What should be taught and accredited?

HMI (DES 1989b) reported impoverished curricula in many schools and units for pupils with EBD and described them as being restricted to the teaching of 'basics' with Science, RE, Humanities and Creative Art often under-represented in timetables. However, sufficient good curricular practice was observed to convince HMI that EBD 'did not impose insuperable barriers to learning' (p. 10) or indeed to the provision of a 'mainstream' curriculum. Perhaps they were cognisant of Weaver's (1968) and Wilson and Evans' (1980) findings that some schools for the maladjusted had long offered CSEs and GCEs as part of their curriculum (although these had tended to be residential rather than day schools). More recently Circular 9/94 (DfE 1994b) stressed that it is the duty of the school for pupils with EBD to provide the full National Curriculum and argued that with creativity and good planning this could be done. As an experienced HMI, it was perhaps predictable that Bull (1995) would praise the introduction of the latter, seeing it as an opportunity to give to pupils with EBD their due entitlement.

However, Orr (1995), a psychotherapist, was not convinced and described the National Curriculum as 'a prescription for failure'. His thinking was more in tune with that of Laslett (1977) who argued that:

> A school for maladjusted children cannot compete with the curricular provision of primary and secondary schools and it should not be expected to. The school exists to make a different kind of educational provision. The children's social and educational readjustment is not going to be achieved by teaching the same subjects as the ordinary school rather differently with rather different teachers. (p. 149)

Cooper *et al.* (1994) also worried that the National Curriculum might make life more difficult and squeeze out imaginative, vocational work to which pupils with EBD could relate and which the DES (1989c) seemed to recommend on the eve of the Education Reform Act. Peagam (1995) and Marchant (1995) were also doubters. While Davies and Landman (1991) found a clear majority of staff in EBD schools generally welcoming the principle of the National Curriculum, many teachers feared that they did not have the teaching skills and resources to deliver some areas of it.

Opinion over the content of the educational curriculum (e.g. O'Reilly 1996) continued to be divided as we conducted our survey and the number of schools judged by OFSTED inspectors to have serious curricular weaknesses mounted. We wondered about the continued relevance of Wilson and Evans' (1980) comment that:

> a smaller range of subjects well taught has more value than an ambitious and wide-ranging programme which does not engage the interests of the pupils. (p. 170)

Had the Dearing reforms to the National Curriculum in 1995, whereby 40 per cent of time for KS4 and 20 per cent of time for KS3 had been 'freed up' from the legal requirement to deliver the National Curriculum, been an endorsement of Wilson and Evans or was it a step backwards towards what one of our respondents described as 'the table tennis curriculum' [M121]?

We asked respondents whether they 'strongly agreed', 'agreed to some extent', 'disagreed' or 'strongly disagreed' with four propositions relating to the National Curriculum:

1. *The majority of this school's teachers accept and support most National Curriculum demands*
   Strongly agree   43%   Disagree   4.5%
   Agree to some extent   50%   Strongly disagree   2.5%   (n = 152)

2. *NC requirements have helped to improve academic achievement in this school*
   Strongly agree   33%   Disagree   9%
   Agree to some extent   55.5% Strongly disagree   2.5%   (n = 153)

3. *NC requirements have made it more difficult to meet pupils' PSE needs*
   Strongly agree   28%   Disagree   23%
   Agree to some extent   45%   Strongly disagree   4%   (n = 154)

4. *NC requirements make it more difficult to manage and motivate our pupils*
   Strongly agree   9%   Disagree   40%
   Agree to some extent   40.5% Strongly disagree   10.5%   (n = 153)

An open-ended question allowed enlargement on the above findings. Many referred to the disadvantages of the National Curriculum:

'There are times in a school day when it appears to be the least appropriate thing on earth for particular pupils.' [M57]

Predictably there were negative comments relating to their ability to delivery personal, social and health education (PSHE). Some saw the National Curriculum as obstructing work on life-skills and addressing individual social needs. Some saw it as making more difficult the delivery of basic literacy and numeracy skills – seen as the pupils' overriding need. A few respondents suggested that the National Curriculum was encouraging a watered down curriculum – a smattering of everything, necessitating less attention to priority areas:

'Too much for EBD children to cope with – recognising that for the majority of EBD children additional time is required in all areas – sacrificing breadth for depth or vice versa.' [M149]

'Would prefer to provide much more 'alternative' style in KS3 and 4 – more parenting skills, counselling, relaxation, PSE group work, etc. It seems pointless to be offering so much of the same curriculum (although different delivery) as our pupils experienced little or no success within mainstream education.' [M160]

However a clear majority had at least some positive comments to make on the National Curriculum. They saw it as a useful framework, facilitating a balanced and broadened curriculum to which all children, including those with EBD, were entitled. It was important in underlining pupils' normality, providing a base from which to prepare children for reintegration (teachers seem to cling to the hope that this will happen). It was also seen to have had a beneficial effect on staff – for example, prompting curriculum development, and raising teacher expectations (particularly for 'old hands'):

'The National Curriculum has certainly forced us to move away from the 'sums, worksheets and minibus' curriculum which existed in the past.' [M162]

'It forms a useful framework for teachers – rather than for pupils.' [N14]

'It has proved managerially useful to help deal with poorly focused teaching.' [M153]

Despite the Dearing reforms there remain worries about volume and degree of mandatory material:

'We feel that Key Stage 4 in particular is very limiting and over prescriptive.' [A34]

'Still overloaded at KS1 and 2.' [M122]

One school urged that the core should be kept but the foundation subjects should be further pruned [M011]. Continuing this theme, allusions were also made to insufficient time being left for Drama, Music, Art, PE and PSHE. These comments are important as in a separate question nominations were sought for subjects viewed as 'having particular therapeutic value'. The responses to this question are give in Table 6.1.

Table 6.1 Subjects viewed as having particular therapeutic value

Art and Craft	PE	English/ Reading	Music
91	53	42	41
Drama	PSHE	Design/ Technology	IT
32	30	27	21
Home Economics	Outdoor Education	Maths	Science
18	15	12	9

Opinion was also elicited on the relative ease or difficulty of meeting the requirements of the National Curriculum and providing Religious Education (RE). Respondents were asked to grade subjects at different Key Stages from 'easy' (awarded one point) through to 'very difficult' (awarded four points). There was a wide range of responses, sometimes though not always, linked to whether a school had a particular subject specialist on its staff. The general shortage of Music, Modern Foreign Language (MFL) and RE specialists (already reported in Chapter 4) seem an obvious explanation for the difficulty schools found in delivering these subjects compared to the relative ease with which English, Art and PE were delivered; there were far more teachers qualified in these subjects. A summary of the findings is given in Table 6.2: it should be noted that this visual representation is not to scale, with the mean scores for most subjects in most Key Stages falling close to 'quite easy'. It does demonstrate how subjects are viewed as becoming either easier or more difficult as pupils progress through Key Stages. It should also be noted that the questionnaire was completed just as MFL became a compulsory subject. Perhaps when schools get used to providing this or have more chance to train staff, it will become easier. At KS4, the mean rating for MFL was slightly closer to 'difficult' than to 'very difficult'. In the case of Information Technology, the difficulty found in providing this occasionally related to lack of modern computer hardware rather than curriculum content or staffing difficulties.

Table 6.2 Ease/difficulty ratings of meeting National Curriculum requirements

Easy	Key Stage 1	Key Stage 2	Key Stage 3	Key Stage 4
	1. Art	1. English	1. Art	1. Maths
	2. English	2. Maths	2. Maths	2. English
	3. Maths	3. Art	3. English	3. PE
Quite easy	4. PE	4. PE	4. PE	
	5. Music	5. Science	5. Geography	
	6. Geography	6. History	6. History	
	7. History	7. Geography		
	8. Science		7. Science	
	9. RE	8. RE		4. Science
	10. Design Technology	9. Information Technology	8. Information Technology	5. Information Technology
	11. Information Technology	10. Design Technology	9. Design Technology	6. Design Technology
			10. RE	
		11. Music		7. RE
Difficult			11. Modern Foreign Languages	
			12. Music	
				8. Music
Very difficult				

In the light of Table 6.2 it is perhaps not surprising that when respondents were asked to nominate National Curriculum areas 'generally regarded as strengths of your school', English topped the number of nominations for each Key Stage, with Art, PE and Maths in the top six for each Key Stage. Less predictable was the finding that Science (rated third at KS3 and second at KS4) was also in the top six for each Key Stage. MFL and RE were least nominated, joined by Music which plummeted from fifth at KS1 to eighth at KS2, to bottom at KS3.

Another perspective on National Curriculum subjects was given when respondents were asked to nominate up to three National Curriculum areas to which their pupils had shown the most positive and most negative responses. Table 6.3 presents the results as well as showing the balance attained by deducting the negative nominations from the positive to produce overall rankings for best classroom response.

Table 6.3 Teachers' assessments of pupils' responses to National Curriculum areas (Figures in the positive and negative columns are the numbers of nominations received)

	Positive	Negative	Balance	Best response
1 = Art	62	5	+ 57	1st
English	62	26	+ 36	4th
3. Science	55	22	+ 33	5th
4. Design Technology	53	8	+ 45	2nd
5. PE	50	10	+ 40	3rd
6. Maths	41	39	+ 2	7th
7. Information Technology	40	12	+ 28	6th
8. Music	18	17	+ 1	8th
9. History	14	23	-9	9th
10. Geography	8	35	- 27	10th
11. MFL	6	49	-43	11th
12. RE	4	53	-49	12th

We also sought respondents' views on why National Curriculum areas elicited good pupil responses. Was this explained by stimulating content or pupils seeing the relevance of subjects to their lives; a combination of these, or 'teacher expertise and confidence in the subject matter'? For all subject nominations combined, the positive responses were ascribed to:

1. Stimulating National Curriculum content   9.0%
2. Pupils see the relevance of the content to their lives   12.4%
3. A mixture of 1 and 2   16.9%
4. Teacher expertise and confidence in their subject matter   61.7%

English was seen as most stimulating and relevant with MFL least, trailing close behind RE. Music, History and Geography also fared badly according to these responses.

The converse question was also asked: What explained negative pupil responses to National Curriculum areas? For all subject nominations combined, the negative responses were attributed to:

1. Inappropriate National Curriculum content   7.4%
2. Pupils do not see relevance of the content to their lives   32.8%
3. A mixture of 1 and 2   27.7%
4. Lack of teacher expertise and confidence in the subject   32.1%
   matter

Predictably MFL and RE received most nominations for inappropriateness and lack of relevance, with Information Technology, Design Technology, Art and PE the least. A relatively high 'irrelevancy quotient' for English is perhaps explained by references in both questionnaire and in our interview data to distinctions made between different parts of the English curriculum. Reading is valued and seen as highly relevant by pupils, while some pupils' practical difficulties in writing and the painful emotional feelings creative writing can induce seem to make other English attainment targets less attractive. Similar sub-divisions were applied to other subjects, for example, Design Technology. In keeping with various commentators on special needs curricula (e.g. the Underwood Committee in relation to the 'maladjusted') the authors were sometimes told that the pupils enjoyed 'hand work' rather than 'head work'. Making things and practical activity had more capacity to motivate and sustain attention than the theoretical aspects of design. Data from the questionnaire and from interviews support the notion that children with EBD tend to prefer to learn through two of Kolb's four learning styles (Kolb 1984): 'concrete experience' and 'active experimentation' rather than 'reflective observation' and 'abstract conceptualisation'. We reflect further on pupils' learning styles in the next section of the chapter.

Data relating to the National Curriculum provide strong evidence that SMTs believe that a good teacher can make any subject interesting to pupils with EBD. Many of our headteachers would agree with the leader of a 'good practice' school:

'The National Curriculum is embodied in statute and I also consider it an entitlement. Our task is therefore to devise approaches and methods to facilitate delivery and not argue over the rights and wrongs.' [M108].

Another spoke in similar vein:

'Slowly learning to "practice fearlessness" with it. We strive hard to work within it, but are no longer slavish in adherence.' [M153]

Schools complaining of what they perceive as the National Curriculum's inflexibility and prescriptiveness might benefit from a similar approach, finding ways to deliver the National Curriculum which match the learning styles of the pupils.

Schools for pupils with EBD also have had a long history of providing a range of nationally accredited courses at KS4 other than GCSEs. DES (1989c), for example, recognised that:

Many of the pupils attending EBD schools have suffered from disrupted schooling and are unlikely to be ready to take the usual examinations at age 16. (p. 6)

If the pupils could not be persuaded to stay on for an extra year's schooling, the DES Circular 23/89 (DES 1989c) continued, then 'consideration should be given to the introduction of alternative curricula such as the Certificate of Pre-Vocational Education (CPVE) and/or the Technical and Vocational Education Initiative (TVEI)' (p. 6). This seems to reflect the practice of many schools where GCSEs are seen as having a part to play but not as an important one as Associated Examing Boards's (AEB) basic skills tests and other more vocational accreditation. In discussion with staff and with pupils at good practice schools, it was commonly argued that GCSEs should be available and as much as possible done to help students tackle these. Pupils viewed them as an important part of 'normal education' and realised that GCSEs tended to have greater 'currency' in the outside world than other tests and examinations (Lovey 1991). However, they also stressed the value of other qualifications to later careers and their potential to provide a focus and a motivator for the final two years of school. It was, however, clearly elucidated by pupils and teachers that they felt it was important that most courses taken have external, nationally recognised accreditation.

One teacher described taking national examinations in terms of the pupil and teacher cooperating, even colluding, to defeat a common enemy – the examiner. Wilson and Evans (1980) made the same point, seeing national examinations as a challenging, motivating force which addressed pupils' complaints that lessons at their special schools were not sufficiently demanding.

McKeon (1997), in part echoing Lovey, reports the deliberations of the London region of the AWCEBD over whether the 'blood, sweat and tears of GCSE courses' might not be worthwhile given the mediocre results which he found in the results for 1996 of over 115 day schools for pupils with EBD in English, Maths and Science. Thirty-two schools (28 per cent) were identified as having no entries or achievements; 61 schools (53 per cent) where students acquired one to four GCSE grades A*–G; 21 (18 per cent) schools where students acquired five or more GCSE grades A*–G, but in only one school did students acquire five or more GCSE grades A*–C.

Historically, residential schools have stressed an examination based curriculum more than day schools (Wilson and Evans 1980) and data from our survey confirmed this. Of 21 schools reporting that one or more of their pupils achieved five GCSEs graded A–G, only one was a maintained day school, one other was an independent day school but the other 19 were all residential schools. Length of the teaching day and the ability to supervise homework could well be relevant factors. On one of the authors' visits, an RSW was observed gently badgering her Year 7 charges in the early evening to complete their homework so that she could allow them out to play. However, it should be noted that an inner city independent day school reported eight pupils achieving five grades A–G and one pupil five A–Cs, showing that it can be done.

More specifically, information produced by our study revealed that:

- The average number of pupils entered and achieving at least one GCSE pass at grades A–G for 1995 was 3.81 pupils (n = 112 schools).
- On average, less than one pupil per school was reported as achieving five grade A–Gs.
- Only six schools reported one or more pupils achieving five grades A–C. One residential school which specialised in admitting pupils of above average ability recorded eight pupils achieving one A–C of which four managed five A–C grades.

It was also clear that McKeon's argument 'for a wider variety of courses for the 14- to 16-year-olds and for other forms of accreditation' (p. 4) is accepted by many schools. A range of non-GCSE courses is being offered across the country, some in National Curriculum subjects but some in practical or alternative areas. The AEB Basic Skills tests, seem to be common fare in many schools. One respondent commented that these were 'good because you cannot fail and always get a certificate' (R20), although this view has to be contrasted with an opposing one reported to the authors by another respondent who said that some pupils feel cheated by their schools when on leaving they discover that these certificates fail to impress potential employers.

Many pupils commonly follow courses in literacy, communications, numeracy, graphicacy, science, health and safety, life skills, and 'world of work', among others, with many achieving passes and sometimes merits. Some schools offer pre-GCSE basic tests. A few schools offer City and Guilds numeracy and English courses and 12 offer the Craft, Design and Technology course. The RSA computer literacy and information technology courses are also offered in some schools for Year 10 pupils as a stepping stone to GCSE Information Systems examinations. Meanwhile for food technology, the St Ivels Home Economics awards, also taught in many mainstream schools, are on offer, as is the basic qualification of the London Chamber of Commerce.

According to our findings, GNVQ is starting to be used in a few schools as a route to practical and vocational qualifications. We observed Year 11 pupils in a residential school, for example, being instructed in painting and decorating and saw the work of students in bricklaying and carpentry as part of GNVQ courses which seemed likely to provide a bridge to higher level courses on offer at FE colleges. Other accredited courses were observed in horticulture and horse-craft.

Our data do not, however, entirely dispel McKeon's concern about the limited success being achieved in GCSE and his pleas for a broader range of alternatives. A case would seem to exist for more respected and accredited vocational courses. Examples of the latter exist but they do not seem to have the 'currency' of GCSEs for pupils, teachers or employers and given the nature of the intake to schools for pupils with EBD (see Chapter 3) success in GCSEs does not seem likely to improve radically. Modular practical courses, such as those currently offered by the Welsh Board, would seem likely to help progress but learning difficulties plus outbursts of behaviour difficulties (we were told of candidates tearing up course work or not attending school on the day of the written examinations) make success very difficult to achieve even here. This is not to say that more opportunities cannot be offered in more schools to pupils who might benefit from GCSE courses: some schools have proved that GCSE success is achievable where proficient teachers have the will.

For GCSE and non-GCSE pupils the Award Scheme Development and Accreditation Network (ASDAN) programmes, which are said to have the support of many higher education institutions (ASDAN 1994), were seen as having value in many of our schools in taking pupils beyond the realms of the National Curriculum and addressing the wider goals of education. The various activities which the youth award scheme encompasses are seen as worthwhile *per se* but also as motivators which help to extend and maintain older pupils' 'ownership' of the curriculum offered by their school.

The disrupted mainstream careers of most EBD pupils, perhaps exacerbated by periods out of school altogether and by a degree of learning difficulty, also impinges on the results of pupils in the standard assessment tasks (SATs) and teacher assessments. As has been noted, a minority of our respondents favour these as an aspect of 'normality therapy' – with one Acting Deputy describing them as:

'*Very* valuable. All have enjoyed them and been proud of their achievements.' [M189].

However, about three quarters of our respondents expressed reservations, often severe, about their value. They disrupt school routines, are said to cause unnecessary stress for pupils and often reinforce pupils' low self-image, making them publicly rehearse their failures while not telling their teachers anything new. It was also noted that they should not be used as an indicator of a school's effectiveness as it is not uncommon for pupils to have to sit SATs shortly after starting their careers in the special school, before they have had time to settle and to start to make measurable educational progress. In the light of the above it was predictable that the details made available to the authors for KS2 SATs and teacher assessments showed pupils commonly performing at levels expected of much younger children.

There was more enthusiasm for compiling records of achievement (ROAs). This was seen as a worthwhile exercise with 96 per cent of schools (n = 120) indicating that ROAs have 'some' or 'a great deal' of value to leavers and 80 per cent of replies indicating a belief that most parents see them as having 'some' or 'a great deal' of value. Similarly, FE tutors and many employers were said to set some store by them.

How should the curriculum be delivered?

HMI (DES 1989b) noted that warm relationships between staff and pupils were common in provision for pupils with EBD, and particularly so in some residential schools. However, this was often where their praise ended: 'It was generally the case that ineffective curricular planning was mirrored in poor teaching and learning' (p. 9). Furthermore, 'ill-judged content of work, poor match of tasks to pupils' capabilities and lack of pace' were frequently noted (p. 10). Comments in a similar vein punctuate many of the OFSTED reports on EBD schools – but not all, effective teaching has been found with the most challenging children. In the best schools this has been observed in nearly every lesson for every class. However, even in schools recommended for special measures, where apparently standards of discipline and organisation were very low, islands of purposeful and tranquil activity were observed by OFSTED inspectors where proficient teachers plied their craft.

Laslett (1977) recorded the surprise of visitors when they saw peaceful classrooms in schools for the maladjusted. He ascribed teacher success not to magical powers but rather to more mundane factors such as structure, consistency, predictability, reliability, 'being there' for the pupils tinged with a degree of sympathy (as well as empathy). Wilson and Evans (1980) also noted tranquil classrooms and found that where a good relationship existed between teacher and pupil, structured, 'small step' teaching with built-in and repeated positive reinforcement could be efficacious. The Schools Council Team did not find widespread expertise in psychodynamic or behaviourist theory – indeed adherence to particular theories sometimes came to be seen as obstacles to the good teaching and care of 'maladjusted' youth (Bridgeland 1971, Whittaker 1979). The Schools Council data indicated little which distinguished 'educational practice with disturbed pupils from what might be considered good educational practice with any pupil' (Dawson 1980, p. 63). Grimshaw with Berridge (1994) drew the same conclusion. Similarly, in the USA, writers have also reported that for the 'emotionally disturbed' good basic teaching techniques do work (Reinert and Huang 1987). Indeed, some of the mechanisms for 'manipulating surface behaviour' advocated by Redl and Wineman (1952), for example, 'proximity control', 'planned ignoring' and 'signal interference', should be part of any teacher's repertoire and are echoed in British mainstream teachers' texts (e.g. Montgomery 1989, Kyriacou 1991). Kounin's (1977) careful analysis of videotapes of practising classroom teachers likewise showed that the factors which helped the teacher to be effective with ordinary children worked equally for most students categorised as emotionally disturbed.

Recent British literature on working with pupils with EBD preaches a similar message (e.g. Galloway and Goodwin 1987, Cooper *et al.* 1994, DfE 1994b). When teachers are well prepared, knowledgeable and skilled in basic classroom management, for example displaying Kounin's 'withitness' (possessing 'eyes in the back of one's head') and paying due respect to the techniques which flow from Smith and Laslett's (1993) four rules of classroom management ('get them in, get them out, get on with it, get on with them'), they are likely to cope well with the demands presented by pupils with EBD.

Their proficiency will be further enhanced if they attend to their pupils' need for differentiation. This has been described by one of the authors (Visser 1993) as 'the very hub of the process of education' and defined as 'the match between the teacher's teaching strategies and the pupil's learning strategies such that the maximum amount of learning can be achieved' (p. 9). This would seem to be particularly important for pupils with EBD.

There will be clear differences in individual learning styles but it would generally seem to be the case, as Wilson and Evans (1980) noted, that 'disturbed children' do not respond well to a permissive Rousseau-esque style where they are free to choose their own learning. Nonetheless,

Cooper *et al.* (1994) amongst others, argue that it is beneficial for pupils to be part of the planning process and make a contribution to monitoring their own performance. Garner (1993), writing on these themes, uses the phrase 'negotiated learning'. Such an approach necessitates verbal communication between teacher and child, thus providing opportunities for talking and listening which are fundamental to the creation of positive relationships and the fostering and maintenance of pupils' ownership of their own learning.

Similarly Lund (1992, 1997) talked of the need to work *with* the pupils rather than directing them in formal pedagogic style. He worried that with the implementation of the National Curriculum formal whole-class teaching might replace the hands-on, experiential, and often cross-subject, project approach which he believed worked best with EBD pupils. As an example, he cited a project focused on the 'Romans' which involved model-making, visits, drama and cookery and where writing was kept to a minimum. Significantly, though, he claimed that teaching by these methods took some 50 per cent longer than more traditional means and that lessons needed to be short and broken down into different activities. Support for his position is provided by Garner (1993) who reported student perceptions that lessons tended to be 'too long'.

The message from the above, and reflected in The Elton Report (DES 1989a) and in government literature (DfE 1994a, 1994b), is that a structured, consultative and individualised style of teaching delivered with creativity and imagination within a wider framework of positive whole-school policies that are permeated with a concern for pupils' personal and social needs (Galloway 1990), not only aids educational progress but also minimises classroom disruption in both mainstream and special school settings. Did the data obtained in our questionnaire and visits to schools confirm this?

In the questionnaire respondents were asked to comment on important factors in pupils' learning. Predictably, perhaps, it was stressed that teachers must be aware of where their pupils *are* and where they can be guided next. They need to know what new learning is within range of their cognitive and affective abilities at a given time and what lies within their 'zone of proximal development' (Cooper 1995, p. 5). An American EBD specialist talked to one of the authors of the importance of the 'Plus One Principle' (Couzens 1997) – taking the pupil just one logical step beyond where he or she is at. Our headteachers reflected an awareness of such thinking:

> 'Pupils need to feel secure in order to attempt work. . . . Work must be within their capability and gradually extended.' [M016]

'Need for routine, structure, predictability, incremental small steps approach.' [N03]

'Pupils tend to rebel against open-ended, exploratory work; need carefully structured work which has built-in success . . . constant encouragement.' [M005]

Short attention span and fear of failure were also commonly mentioned:

'Distractibility . . . children expect to fail. Subterfuge – trick them into success if necessary.' [A11]

'Short attention span – requires stimulation in short bursts.' [M131]

'Need for variety, given short attention span.' [N03]

'They need reinforcement and repetition.' [A34]

Tailoring tasks to pupil interests was advised:

'Frequent need to relate to own immediate interests and concerns.' [M162]

Having a variety of approaches to use was seen as an advantage:

'Be prepared to deviate – having three routes to your goal/teaching objective is valuable. The pupils can meander under guidance. EBD views are important as well – let them trial their ideas.' [M204]

Allusions were also made to pupils' difficulties with writing and 'reluctance to put pen to paper' [M035], suggesting the 'need to work from a practical base'. [M073]

The authors' visits included some classroom observations involving primary-aged children through to Year 11 pupils. We saw highly effective and less successful practice, as is recorded in many OFSTED reports, and were left agreeing with the theory outlined at the start of this section. Committed, organised, knowledgeable teachers are as effective with pupils with EBD as with other children – although they will probably have to work harder, sometimes 'smarter', making more sacrifice and more consciously attempting to address pupils' expressive or affective needs to achieve success. We did not see special techniques but saw, to use the OFSTED phrase, 'secure subject knowledge' as well as much evidence of warm relationships, mutual respect, firmness and all the qualities required of effective teachers, already described in Chapter 4.

In the questionnaire we sought further opinion on approaches to the classroom task. In the main our findings, summarised in Table 6.4, confirm the results of earlier research, particularly that of Wilson and

111

Evans (1980) on the importance of structuring learning to build pupils' self-image and strong hints, confirmed in our interview data, that education itself, particularly catching up in the 'basic subjects', can be viewed as a type of therapy. To establish a rank order, four points were awarded to 'very important' responses, through to one point for 'unimportant'.

Table 6.4 Approaches to managing and motivating pupils ranked according to perceived importance (n ranges from 151 to 153)

	Very important %	Important %	Quite important %	Not important %
1. Improving pupils' self-image by helping them succeed.	96	3	1	0
2. Helping pupils 'catch up' in basic language and number skills.	76	19	5	0
3. Challenging but appropriate curricula expectations.	61	33	6	0
4. Wide curricula access through differentiated teaching.	54	36	9	1
5. Well planned individual educational programmes.	59	26	12	3
6. Structured personal and social education programme.	47	40	13	0
7. Creative work in the arts.	35	43	22	1
8. Frequent pupil involvement in planning their own learning.	21	34	35	9
9. Frequent use of inf. technology in many curriculum areas.	15	36	45	4
10. Cross-curricular topic work.	7	22	47	24
11. Allowing pupils substantial choice in what they study.	2	17	44	37

The lukewarm response which was evident for cross-curricular topic work is perhaps linked to a general preference for a traditional, mainstream-type timetable with discrete lessons provided in 35 or 40 minute periods for pupils in KS3 and KS4. Our study of many timetables showed that occasionally a school opts for longer double-periods or operates a primary school model of four extended periods on the grounds of cutting down the movement of pupils. However, the demands of the National Curriculum and pressure from OFSTED inspectors to have individual subjects taught by specialist teachers would seem to have pushed schools towards a mainstream pattern. The number of secondary schools where it was felt more important for a generalist teacher with a good relationship with the children to offer a range of subjects would seem to be diminishing, although our data do not give a definitive verdict on this.

The norm would seem to be one teacher to a class of about eight, perhaps aided for some of the time by an LSA, teaching a traditional length lesson but teachers break down that period into short, manageable sections suited to individual pupil's needs and inject pace and variety within the confines of the specialist subject topic. There are, of course, times when classes combine to create sufficient numbers for PE. A freer use of time and groupings was observed as three classes in a primary school combined when a local authority science adviser undertook some work with the children as a prelude to a staff training session.

One exception to the mainstream pattern seems to be Friday afternoons, commonly used for rewarding pupils scoring highly on a school's points system via activities programmes and are a time when some pupils start their journey home for the weekend. Monday mornings too sometimes begin with a staff meeting and a later start to lessons. A few schools also create some space for school and group meetings.

The dilemma of finding time for activities specifically targeted at pupils' social and affective needs while allocating sufficient time to the compulsory components of the National Curriculum is not easy to resolve. However, it should be noted that a similar dilemma predated the introduction of the National Curriculum. This is seen in the standard allocation to subject areas of school time found by Dawson (1980). It seems that many schools then opted for a mainstream-type curriculum. The mean figure for time devoted to 'fundamental skills' was 39 per cent; humanities, 13 per cent; 'handicrafts', 8 per cent and sciences, 7 per cent. Fifteen per cent was devoted to creative arts (this included writing) and 12 per cent to 'PE and allied activities' leaving only 6 per cent for 'others'. PSE would seem to have been delivered through other subjects and out of class hours. Talk about widespread movement in the last decade from a counselling and table tennis curriculum to a mainstream one may be overdone. However, Weaver's (1968) observation that many headteachers of that era did not see it as important to adhere to formal timetables may explain apparent discrepancies between Dawson's evidence and views expressed to the authors. Perhaps the tendency to ignore timetables persisted into the 1990s.

General approaches to behaviour management

If children are to be 'available for learning' (Greenhalgh 1994, p. 1) then what happens as they get up in the residential school, or on the way to school in the taxi or bus, or in break times or at lunch times or the evening care hours can settle or upset children, can diminish or increase their desire to apply themselves during formal lessons. The literature (e.g. Wilson and Evans 1980) suggests that there are approaches which best address pupils' needs and thereby help to motivate them and make the management of their challenging behaviour easier both in and outside the classroom. We chose to explore 12 such approaches based upon our review of the literature. On the supplementary care questionnaire, we asked the same questions but only used the responses when we knew that the respondents were Heads of Care or other senior care staff. The summary of our findings is given in Table 6.5.

Table 6.5 Meeting the needs of pupils ranked by teacher-respondents according to perceived importance (n ranges from 141 to 153)

	Very important %	Important %	Quite important %	Not important %
1. = Frequent encouragement and praise.	92	5	2	1
Clear expectations and firm, consistent discipline.	91	6	3	0
3. A well-established daily routine.	89	9	1	1
4. Caring, long-lasting relationships between staff and pupils.	76	20	3	1
5. = Helping children to express their feelings appropriately.	63	30	7	1
Staff who listen to children and reflect back their feelings.	65	28	6	1
7. Key-worker or named person for each child.	41	24	14	21
8. Group discussions/meetings with skilled staff.	27	38	27	8
9. Touch/holding children by staff to comfort/ease tantrums.	22	37	30	11
10. Regular individual counselling with qualified counsellor/therapist.	11	26	38	25
11. 'Sorting out' pupils' EBD before stressing their education.	12	16	20	52
12. Use of drug therapy (other than for the control of epilepsy).	3	3	20	74

Rankings given by 43 Heads of Care or senior RSWs were similar, with all rating 'frequent praise and encouragement' as 'very important'; 91 per cent rating 'a well-established routine' and 84 per cent 'clear expectations and firm, consistent discipline' as 'very important'. A higher rating was given to both 'group discussions/meetings with skilled staff' and 'keyworker or named person for each pupil' with the same percentage, 86 per cent, saying they rated each of these as 'very important' or 'important'. Similarly 'touch/holding' was seen as more important with some 79 per cent seeing it as important or very important. Individual counselling and drug therapy received similar ratings to those ascribed by teacher-respondents. Professional training and contrasting experience perhaps explain the differences while the similarity in many answers points to the convergence of philosophies within many SMTs, facilitating the consistency of approach which tends to characterise proficient schools. This convergence of views does not come as a surprise to the authors after meeting headteachers, deputy headteachers and Heads of Care on visits to schools.

The responses in Table 6.5 seem consistent with views recorded earlier in this book. In terms of the theoretical underpinnings of working with pupils with EBD the answers suggest that most staff operate at an interface between behaviourist and psychodynamic positions. Social learning, positive reinforcement and clarity of expectation are deemed essential to provide stability to the pupils' lives and our visits provided clear evidence of staff implementing behaviourist principles, including on occasion the regular use of 'time-out' rooms. Staff clearly believed in the need for adult direction and provision of structure, but what they practised was 'behaviourism with heart'.

Boundary setting is seen to assist pupils with EBD but the buffers, as indicated above (see 'rubber boundaries'), should be forgiving, allowing for a child's idiosyncrasies. Rules should generally be consistent and understood and followed by all, yet should retain flexibility and be interpreted with individual needs in mind. When transgressions occur, the behaviour and not the child should be condemned and rejected. The reasons for the child's actions should be investigated. The pupil has the right to express his or her views, to have staff available who can listen, comfort and advise, sometimes directively, sometimes non-directively.

Group meetings where pupils can make their views heard – a practice associated with the psychodynamic perspective – were viewed as important by three-quarters of the respondents. In contrast, formal regular counselling from trained therapists is a luxury no longer on the menu of most schools. Even if it were, our interview data suggest that often it

115

would not be welcomed: it was commonly seen as sufficient for teachers and RSWs and other support staff to offer a sympathetic ear and to talk to pupils as they shared each others' 'life-space'. Cooper *et al.* (1994) suggest that by 'listening and talking' staff were operating at the simplest 'outer' level of psychodynamic theory but to be effective this has to be based on good relationships: staff must be significant others to the pupils if the latter are to value talking to them.

We observed staff at all levels of the organisation matching up to these conditions: pupils sought their company at any time of the day. When mealtimes had ended, pupils would linger, seeking an opportunity to have a quick word with a favoured member of staff, or volunteer to carry out a small job as an excuse to be close to the staff member and able to talk. On the playground at lunch time they would be observed joking with staff. In this way the latter build up a reserve of mutual goodwill to help both child and adult get through later bad times together, with the child more willing to accept the control of the adult and the will of the school. Perhaps, conversely, the adult and the school are more willing to forgive the transgressions or challenges of the child whom they like and genuinely wish to help. Even the 'punishments', for example the end-of-day detention observed by one of the authors, could be both an instrument of control but at the same time a chance to further relationships and to explore why 'bad behaviour' had occurred and how the child might react differently on future occasions. A respected and liked senior teacher was seen carrying out these dual roles. There was a mutual shaking of heads and a wry joking exchange as a senior pupil entered this teacher's detention yet again and as he carried out his assigned task there were brief verbal exchanges interspersed with the teacher offering help.

Addressing Maslow's needs of love and belongingness can sometimes require an appropriate use of physicality – the arm round a shoulder, holding a young pupil's hand. Rutman (1992, p. 200) quoted Keating: 'Touch is not only nice, it's needed.' King (1993) preached a similar message. Appropriate physicality would seem to be a natural part of creating warm, positive relationships, particularly but not exclusively for younger pupils. The authors observed primary-aged pupils snuggling up to favourite care workers and teachers at morning assembly and headteachers instinctively touching senior pupils' arms. Such actions seem entirely appropriate, particularly in the aftermath of an upset when 'emotional first aid' (Redl 1966) is required. Official, post-1989 Children Act, guidance distinguishes permitted from banned forms of physical contact (i.e. corporal punishment): 'The use of "holding" which is commonly used, and often helpful, containing experience for a distressed child is not excluded.' (Department of Health 1991a, p. 17). The many allegations apparently made against staff (see Chapter 5) in the early 1990s, help to explain what the AWCEBD (1997) newsletter described as the damaging 'taboo on tenderness' (p. 7). Regretably some interviewees clearly feel safer avoiding any kind of physical contact with pupils, even when they know a child would benefit from this, for fear of allegations. It was therefore reassuring that many senior staff still saw the use of touch and physical holding as a necessary part of the worker's repertoire, subject, of course, to close knowledge of a child's background. If there is a history of abuse or allegations then staff are right to be circumspect.

We now move to another response reported in Table 6.5. Begg (1982), echoing Underwood (Ministry of Education 1955) and Beedell (1993), wrote in relation to new pupils in a therapeutic community:

> Not only is there no pressure on a boy to attend classes; they are forbidden to him. Even if he expresses a desire to get involved in school-work, he is not allowed to do so. The rationale for this approach is that minds as troubled as those of the boys coming to High Plains, are not ready for learning. Time is needed for the 'kinks' to be straightened out before meaningful learning can take place. (p. 114)

The notion that inner turmoil needed 'sorting out' before education could begin was not in line with the views of most of our respondents for nearly all of their pupils: however 28 per cent of them saw this as 'important' or 'very important'. In interview, senior staff said that they viewed the classroom experience as a vehicle for assisting the 'sorting out': it was necessary to tackle the emotional and behavioural difficulties at the same time as proceeding to address educational needs. However, a few senior staff did make a distinction between the vast majority of children with EBD and a few at the psychiatric end of the continuum for whom education would not be a priority. These they would have preferred to have seen placed in therapeutic communities.

In the light of current controversy about ADHD we did not include a question about it directly but did ask one about 'the use of drug therapy'. We made the assumption that most respondents would make a connection with the prescription of methylphenidate (e.g.'Ritalin') for pupils said to have ADHD but if that was the case it seems that a clear majority do not see 'drug therapy' as contributing usefully to the management and motivation of pupils with EBD. The returns suggest a fifth of respondents see it as having a place – perhaps as part of a multi-modal approach for some pupils? A few respondents expressed strong opposition to the use of drugs on the margin of the survey form. On the authors' visits to schools, contrasting views were expressed. On one occasion a headteacher was strongly against the use of 'Ritalin' while his deputy was for it. An acting headteacher was unperturbed by the fact that half of a class in his school were taking the drug and said that if some of the pupils were not, the school could not hold them. Another staff member alluded to the problems of parents unevenly administering drugs to their child, claiming this made for contrasting behaviour – sometimes excessively volatile, at other times over-somnolent. One of the authors observed a child said to have ADHD displaying these extremes at the dinner table and in class. While we met 'supporters', our data suggest continuing doubts exist among many teachers and care staff. This is in stark contrast to the practice briefly observed by the authors in American residential treatment centres for students categorised as both SED (Severely Emotionally Disturbed) and ADHD, where medication seems to be administered as a matter of course to the vast majority of students.

Behaviour management: policy and practice

How did the beliefs described in the previous section transpose into the schools' systems for both class and care situations? Again, drawing upon the relevant literature, we wished to probe the opinion of staff on a range of relevant topics. A question in the main questionnaire was replicated in the supplementary care questionnaire in order that we might identify differences in response between senior teaching and senior care staff. In those cases where headteachers answered the care questionnaire, their answers were not used. Our findings from the main survey form are summarised in Table 6.6.

The responses of Heads of Care and other senior RSWs produced similar answers but with some differences. Perhaps predictably, given the nature of care work (less structured class work and more potential for 'blow-ups' requiring physical intervention), Heads of Care gave the highest rating to the need for a detailed written physical restraint policy with 73.2 per cent saying this was 'very useful' and a further 24.4 per cent rating it 'useful'. Similarly, given the impact of social services inspections/Children Act on thinking about care in residential schools, it was not surprising that Heads of Care should give a higher rating to schools' complaints procedures with 97.5 per cent saying this was either 'very useful' or 'useful' compared with 73.8 per cent for teacher-respondents. Care workers seemed slightly less enamoured with behaviourist systems, with 78.1 per cent rating them as 'very useful' or 'useful' compared with 85.7 per cent of teacher-respondents.

Table 6.6 Relative usefulness of school-wide approaches to behaviour management as perceived by respondents (ranked in overall order of perceived importance)

	Very useful %	Useful %	Quite useful %	Little use %	n =
1. Extra staff to look after pupils wandering/ejected from class.	73	19	4	4	82
2. = A detailed written behaviour management policy.	62	30	6	2	136
Sanctions/deterrents agreed and applied by all staff.	62	30	8	0	133
4. = Incentives agreed and applied by all staff.	60	31	8	1	134
A written detailed physical restraint policy.	67	21	9	3	122
6. A behaviour management system based on points or tokens.	55	31	11	3	119
7. Community meetings where pupils express their views.	40	37	20	3	90
8. A complaints procedure clearly understood by pupils.	35	39	15	11	103
9. Children's council/court to discuss misbehaviour.	24	28	34	14	50

The most highly rated practice was the ability of schools to offer a back-up service to class teachers when pupils either absented themselves or were asked to leave class. The idea of the 'crisis teacher' has a long provenance (see Reinert and Huang 1987) in the USA and it would seem to be a well-established role for senior teachers and care staff working daytime hours to act as 'sweeper' when problems arise which class teachers cannot handle unaided.

Written policies guiding whole-school systems

Appreciation of the value of detailed, written behaviour management policies was widespread with 85 per cent of respondents reporting that they had these. Samples of such policies sent to the authors indicate comprehensive documents spreading outwards from a mission statement to those which covered many aspects of behaviour. The theme was usually 'prevention is better than crisis intervention'. Some policies included descriptions of the theories of behaviour and methods emanating from these, working presumably on the principle that greater staff understanding should make for more appropriate responses. The emphasis was often on fostering of good behaviour before concentrating on how to cope with the 'bad' or challenging. Approximately 80 per cent of respondents also claimed that their school had school-wide systems of sanctions and deterrents as well as incentives, which had been agreed and were applied by all staff. In the course of our visits it was not possible to check in detail whether systems were actually applied by all and we did encounter staff showing varying degrees of enthusiasm for their school's systems. However, we heard and observed sufficient to suggest that staff in proficient schools have been involved in the creation and monitoring of school-wide systems of rewards and sanctions, seeing the importance of the consistency that these bring and the potential for aiding pupils' behaviour and general development; consequently, a majority of staff felt a sense of ownership of them and put their heart into implementing them.

Sometimes, respondents said that they had been pushed into extending systems because the pupils requested it. More than once we were told that a reward system developed for younger pupils had been extended to later year groups for this reason; the pupils had thought it fairer and perhaps still hankered after the tangible rewards associated with the policies.

Points mean prizes!

Given the broad provenance of EBD schools and the varied backgrounds of the staff, the existence of points and tokens systems in the sample schools was perhaps to be expected but the authors were still surprised that 70 per cent of respondents reported that they operated these. On the authors' visits, we observed points scores displayed prominently on school walls, star charts on classroom boards and heard staff reporting back, albeit sensitively, to groups of children how many points they had achieved at morning assembly or in the final period of the afternoon. It was common for points to be awarded for promptness, for interpersonal relationships, for attitude to work, for helpfulness and other attributes for every lesson and for break and lunch times and for behaviour in the evening care hours. These were often linked to colour-coded level systems and the enjoyment of 'privileges' or increasing levels of independence (for example, freedom to walk into the neighbouring town). They often also led to prize-giving ceremonies sometimes on a weekly, sometimes on a monthly, basis. They were used to determine the children who had access to activities on Friday afternoons, who went on evening trips, for example to the swimming baths, and who qualified for special outings at the end of a half-term to a theme park or to McDonalds. Occasionally they were linked to substantial bonuses of weekly pocket money.

Extrinsic rewards are clearly seen as having an important part to play in achieving stable, well-ordered communities but also as a means of furthering pupils' social and academic development and a highly visible way of recognising success and building self-esteem.

Karen Vander Ven complained of the prevalence of such systems in the USA:

> Like strange bacteria that can thrive only by being attached to a particular host, they almost seem to float through the air, drop and install themselves in settings for children and youth, spreading and coming to serve as the focal point for the ideology, activity, and rules for daily living. (cited in Barnes and Barnes 1996, p. 54)

She claimed, somewhat strangely, given the visits she has made to this country, that these were a uniquely North American phenomenon which appalled trained European 'socialpedagogs'. Her fellow countryman, Whittaker (1979), a convert from a neo-Freudian standpoint argued otherwise. He conceded that systems could be cold and mechanical, if divorced from other theoretical standpoints, but saw behaviourist approaches as very useful in developing social skills in a range of areas for young people in residential settings. McMaster (1982) gave British backing to behaviourism guiding work with troubled youth and this point of view would seem to prevail in the majority of schools in our survey.

Seasoned exponents of a behaviourist approach would probably concede possible disadvantages of points and tokens systems. They can lead to 'reward inflation'; they can be manipulated by pupils and indeed by staff; they can create a dependency culture which makes the development of intrinsic pro-social behaviour more difficult to foster. We picked up hints of these tendencies on our school visits.

Sanctions

At odds with the position of some 'pioneers' (Dockar-Drysdale 1968), we found that punishment is also seen as having a role to play in special schools for children with EBD as much as in mainstream schools. This no longer amounts to the beatings condemned by Wills (1960) and there would seem to be wide recognition among the senior staff we interviewed that, even if the law allowed it, severe and regular forms of punishment do not produce lasting changes in behaviour. In a mainstream context the punishment which characterised 'coercive schools' (Reynolds and Sullivan 1979, cited in Cooper *et al.* 1994) undermines the development of positive school ethos. However, in our schools sanctions such as stopping a child going on a trip or staying in at break or attending an after school detention were seen as valuable. Sanctions in a number of schools were linked to variations of Canter's Assertive Discipline (see Bush and Hill 1993, for its application in EBD schools and Hanko 1993, for a critique). Commonly, a first warning for misbehaviour was forgiven but second, third and further warnings were linked to an increasing tariff of sanctions leading to referral to the SMT. These systems were generally operated in every class in a school, although we sensed from the fading and torn rule-charts in some classrooms that they were embraced with varying degrees of enthusiasm by teachers. Some staff clearly worried that systems such as these made the flexibility of response which is sometimes required for pupils with EBD more difficult.

In schools with less formal discipline systems, stopping pupils going on trips or missing favoured on-site activities, were common practices. In line with recent Scottish research (Sanders and Hendry 1997), staff reporting bad behaviour to pupils' parents was seen as an effective sanction.

Interviews with senior staff as well as open-ended questionnaire responses clearly showed that staff believed sanctions to be necessary but they were seen to work best if they were based on positive relationships between adult and pupil. Punishments were an outward and easily understood sign of the significant adult's inner disappointment. They showed other children that 'something was being done' about behaviour which might disturb them: as one deputy headteacher noted: 'They don't mind acting out themselves, but they hate it when the others do'. Pupils also see that sanctions are also a part of 'normalisation': pupils in mainstream schools and children at home face punishments if they knowingly misbehave.

Less confident staff tend to see the ability to give out specific sanctions as a necessary prop – but therein lies potential danger. They might place ill-founded faith in the efficacy of punishment and resort increasingly to its use. 'In no way did successful control seem related to severe measures' (Wilson and Evans 1980, p. 161). Severe or frequent use of sanctions is likely to exacerbate these staffs' problems with the pupils and obstruct relationship formation, as Dockar-Drysdale (1968) noted.

The philosophy underlying the dictum 'four positives to one negative' cannot be ignored. Indeed its application was much in evidence on our visits to the good practice schools. It was observed at individual level with frequent signs of encouragement given by RSWs, LSAs, secretaries, cooks, handymen and teachers to pupils. It was also seen at institutional level with praise and recognition, for example, being given to pupils at assemblies.

The value of the group gathering for this purpose was also clearly seen. Perhaps influenced by Laslett (1977), Begg (1982) and others, some staff saw the potential of group work for fostering personal growth, promoting good relationships and sometimes utilising peer group pressures to bring about behavioural change. Bringing the whole school community together and using it as a vehicle for staff and pupils to explore ideas and pass positive, as well as the occasional negative, comment on other children, was recognised in many of our schools. Nearly half our sample reported such gatherings were held in their schools, with a larger number seeing their potential (see Table 6.5). A few replies to other questions suggested a growing use of 'Circle Time' (Mosley 1991, Curry 1997) as a vehicle for positive small-group work. Groups were also seen as vehicles for expression of 'consumer' views on school systems – a legitimate and sensible means for children to air grievances or to contribute to the review of school policy.

Group work might help to minimise the need to use a school's more formal complaints procedures. The prominence given to these in the post-1989 Children Act guidance (Chapter 5, Department of Health 1991a) is reflected in the importance attached to them by the social service inspectors who visit independent schools and who might in future be required to inspect maintained residential schools for pupils with EBD. It therefore seemed important to probe respondents' views on the need for such procedures. Nearly three-quarters of respondents saw them as 'very useful' or 'useful' and these views were reflected in our observation of complaints procedures pinned to care unit walls. Official advice is that procedures 'should be uncomplicated, accessible to those who might wish to use them, understood by all members of staff and should reflect the need for confidentiality at all stages' (Department of Health 1991a, p. 82). Whether this is best achieved by requiring extensive written documentation is a moot point – it might be that verbal promotion of children's rights in this area may be more meaningful.

The least favoured approach for both teachers and care workers was the practice of a few pioneer schools where children sat in 'courts' and passed judgement on their peers (Bridgeland 1971) and which has been resurrected recently (Elliott 1991) with reference to bullying. Only 20 per cent of respondents said that they operated a court or council with only 50 respondents expressing a view on its usefulness. Of these just over half thought they were 'useful' or 'very useful'.

Life outside directed class time

Our respondents generally agreed that the time spent in formal lessons must be the centre of school life but they also stressed the importance of time pupils spent outside the classroom. In line with the Underwood Report (Ministry of Education 1955) and Wilson and Evans (1980) they noted the potential of all the hours of the day for social and educational learning and for emotional growth. There are, however, different views on how this is best achieved. Is a highly structured, adult-directed timetable, keeping pupils busy from rising through to bedtime, the right way to go about it? Or is it more appropriate to allow children time to relax, to play, to be themselves and even to escape adult supervision and to choose how they use their time (Beedell 1970). Millham *et al.* (1975) found both perspectives represented in the approved schools of the late 1960s, noting clear differences between 'training schools' characterised, particularly for junior aged pupils, by constant, adult-motivated and controlled activity and more child-centred, social work approaches with much talk and counselling but far less programming of the pupils by the staff. They concluded that the former tended to induce a better response from pupils. Wilson and Evans (1980) found similar different emphases for the schools for the maladjusted a decade later.

Both approaches can clearly be taken to extremes. The 'training schools' can be militaristic establishments where the needs of the individual are submerged in systems designed for ease of group management and where unnecessary customs evolve for the benefit of staff – enforced silence at meals, cleaning teeth to numbers (Wills 1971), queuing up for showers, lining up and marching. The end-product could be institutionalised automatons incapable of independent decision-making. Sydney Turner, the first inspector of Victorian industrial schools, used to stress that voluntary rather than enforced good behaviour must be pursued, as only the former would last (Carlebach 1967). On the other hand, some child-centred establishments were found by Millham *et al.* (1975) to descend into laissez-faire regimes, with bored children, prone to running away and getting into trouble, sometimes with staff largely losing control. We saw nothing resembling these extremes in the course of our visits and it is to be hoped, almost a decade after the 1989 Children Act, that the extremes no longer exist. However, OFSTED reports on some 'special measures' schools do refer to pupils who are often bored and staff who are hardly in control.

Significantly, too, a number of our respondents commented on the need for structure and stressed the need to supervise and control the behaviour of their pupils almost ceaselessly. One headteacher identified the provision of 'a structured back to back day' (M087) as a significant feature of his school. Another reported that when he was persuaded to take on the leadership of a school which had slipped into near-chaos, he had found it necessary to ensure that pupils were escorted from A to B, that staff were out in the playground at lunch times and that pupils were always kept in view. Yet another, similarly charged with bringing round an out-of-control, laissez-faire, psychodynamically-oriented school reported that he had consciously moved offices, installed glass panels in walls and cut off the branches of trees and cleared undergrowth, erected an eight foot fence so that there was nowhere for the pupils to escape to or to hide from adult view. In other schools we saw video cameras in corridors and electric alarms which went off if doors were opened in the night. Is a policy of almost total supervision necessary and what are the ethical bounds?

In the schools mentioned in the last few sentences, we were impressed by the relaxed, positive relationships which existed between staff and pupils, the quality of education and care and the state of the physical provision. As we sat down to breakfast in one of the schools the children obviously felt free to talk and later one Year 11 pupil compared the school very favourably to three other schools he had attended. Here, as in all the good practice schools visited by the authors, and apparently those we have read about in both social service and OFSTED inspection reports, an appropriate balance had been achieved. There was warmth and caring which the consciously imposed structure and simple but well-established routines made easier.

Senior management teams in these highly organised schools, whether consciously or unwittingly, had apparently imbibed the message of writers associated with psychodynamic and humanist perspectives (e.g. Bettelheim 1950, Dockar-Drysdale 1968, Trieschman et al. (1969) and more recently Vander Ven 1991 and Kahan 1994) in utilising the school milieu to provide good quality primary care which addressed lower order physiological needs and at the same time creating opportunities to address higher order needs such as self-esteem (Maslow 1943, 1970).

Basic daily routines such as getting children up or putting them to bed can be used by skilful staff to pursue these goals (see Trieschman et al. 1969, Berry 1975, Maier 1981 and Cole 1986) but given concerns for privacy, these were not areas which the researchers could easily observe.

125

However, we were welcomed at mealtimes in various schools. How food is shared is held up by writers quoted in the previous paragraph as presenting opportunities for the delivery of quality child care and we did participate in some family-style meals which could be viewed as therapeutic experiences. There was talk and controlled humour, there was turn-taking, there was gentle coaxing of manners. However, in an era of TV dinners and fast-food, the importance attached to the sharing of food in traditional style may now have an old-fashioned ring. Certainly some of our good practice schools had opted for cafeteria-style feeding with staggered starting and finishing times and a plethora of chips and sandwiches in plastic containers and individual drink packs. We were told that this approach has been adopted to lessen the management problems of having a large number of volatile pupils who can do nasty things to each others' food in one room for an extended period; but at what cost was this to the emotional development of fragmented children who lack a sense of belonging and value?

The main questionnaire sought further information about arrangements for lunch supervision. The Elton Committee (DES 1989a), writing in the aftermath of teacher strikes and withdrawal of goodwill, only found it possible to *recommend* that teachers play a part in this, noting that it tended to aid the achievement of good ethos. The questionnaire replies confirmed by our observations show teachers in many schools playing a very active part. In about 25 per cent of schools (n = 154) 'all' or 'nearly all' teachers were reported to sit with the children and most schools rostered a proportion of teachers to sit with children each day. In addition, there would usually be a significant number of RSWs or LSAs present. Our visits suggested that it was common practice for there to be a member of staff to each table. Only once did we observe a deputy headteacher struggling unaided to control a rowdy lunch time while most of the staff sheltered in a distant staff room.

At another school, where we were told that it was a common for the food to be ready late, there was scarcely time for pupils to finish their food and any chance of 'seconds' was denied because, to ease discipline problems, the lunch break had been shortened. Eating had become an undignified scramble as pupils were bundled rapidly back into class without opportunity to play outside.

Other schools had also telescoped the school day, cutting out all or nearly all breaks because of the behaviour management problems which could punctuate these times. If some schools can involve their teachers and support staff to provide full supervision, often offering a range of indoor and outdoor activities, why cannot others? Clearly it can be done despite the perceived increasing difficulty of pupils and the obvious need for staff to have a break. We observed happy, semi-structured dinner hours, with staff offering a range of activities while other children chose to 'let off steam' running around in the playground or gym as they would in most mainstream schools.

We recognised too one headteacher's annoyance when he caught two members of staff standing together chatting at break time as an incident occurred in a distant corner but noted with interest that his planned response was either to remind the staff that 'the most effective supervision is done on the move' (Laslett 1977, p. 91) or to become actively involved, offering an activity to the pupils. This headteacher was not on the verge of abolishing lunch break.

Many schools reported allowing pupils access to quiet havens indoors as well as outdoor play areas during lunch breaks, following the advice of Elton (DES 1989a). In some schools, senior pupils were allocated their own common room, which was supervised from a distance, allowing them chance to escape adult supervision.

In short we saw varying degrees of freedom allowed to pupils at lunch times ranging from

'The girls organise themselves and us.' [M215]

through

'Full activity programme on offer at all times – little chance to become "EBD".' [R18]

and

'Flexi-breaks are held: teachers remain with own groups. Varied activities; coffee/lounge facility in each classroom.' [N14]

or

'Children earn playtime by task completion. Options: competitions, lego, dressing up, craft, roller skating in hall and outside play. (Staff ratio) 1:7 every playtime. c.8 adults on duty.' [M30]

to

'No midday playtime.' [M142]

We also found variety in how pupils moved through buildings. In some, children were kept on a very tight lead, with teachers and RSWs carefully escorting groups from class or care unit to assembly or dining hall. The headteacher of a school which had evolved from an approved school noted how social service inspectors hated the way his pupils, some aged over 16, were still lined up in the gym, before being escorted to lessons. He said it was a tradition which had helped to maintain good order for over a generation and he had no intention of altering it. We watched the good humour which punctuated this particular ritual, which was also used to present an outdoor pursuit award to a pupil. In another school care staff stood at strategic points watching children as they walked from lesson to lesson. Here again, some staff and the previous headteacher had worked in approved schools/CHEs. Other schools were far more relaxed about pupil movement. It would seem that 'good practice' varies from situation to situation depending on traditions, design of building, age and maturity of group and the philosophy of the school. Thus, systems are probably best determined locally. If pupils are happy with regimented approaches and these are offset by warm caring relationships and good care and education, and if these do indeed reduce disruption and friction at transitions then why should their routines be altered?

Recent research in relation to the disaffected (Sanders and Hendry 1997) has found that young people want teachers who can control them. This is entirely consistent with the views we encountered in our research and also with the findings of earlier work (e.g. Milham *et al.* 1975, Wilson and Evans 1980). Redl's (1966) concept of the 'great ego-supportive power of traditionalised routine' to which reference was made above is also relevant here. Routine can help to provide the sense of security and belonging that pupils with EBD need. It can, as Studt (1968) noted, be a 'benign external fabric which subtly supports and directs the child towards satisfactions achieved through acceptable behaviour' (p. 5). However, routines and rituals can go too far or may be perceived as pointless time-fillers which dominate school life. One of the authors remembers working on a weekend care team in the mid 1970s with a deputy headteacher who had worked in Home Office approved schools for many years. Two hours each Saturday morning were devoted by the 75 boys to polishing and repolishing their shoes to a standard which would have made a regimental sergeant major smile. This is probably the kind of routine Kahan (1994) had in mind when she called for time spent on routines to be kept to a minimum although she does write that 'some structured use of time gives order to the day' (p. 102).

She proceeds to give advice on how to provide for the care hours. Following Beedell (1970), she believes that generally young people in residential care should be free to decide for themselves how they use their spare time:

> An imposed structure of 'uplifting' activities is unlikely to be as helpful to children and young people as encouragement to use their time

constructively. Adolescents especially like to spend time with their friends and should not be obliged to undertake structured activities in what they see as their leisure time. (p. 102)

But, she also recognises that in residential special schools, activity programmes have a valuable place. She hints that it is easier to provide worthwhile ones in these settings than in small vertically grouped children's homes – and perhaps pupils who find relationships with their fellows more difficult need activity programmes more. 'Good practice' would seem to require the achievement of balance and that there should be free time. Our study of timetables and our observations indicated that the latter is usually provided before, and immediately after, tea and after 7 p.m. as well as during the weekends.

At the same time, to avoid boredom turning into 'acting out' a wide-range of activities should be offered. Morgan (1993) discovered that his small sample of pupils attending residential EBD schools rated the provision of a range of voluntary activities as one of the most attractive features of boarding life. In a school for 50 or more pupils with a care team of ten, it should be possible to provide challenge and interest. If teachers are also offering extensions to their daytime work, for instance in Art or on computers or in outdoor pursuits, then it should be possible to engage the attention of most pupils. There may be initial resistance but hopefully this will be replaced by satisfaction and pride of achievement – particularly if the video has been set to record favoured 'soaps' which can be saved for later in the evening.

Our views on activity programmes are offered in the light of the many years one of us was involved in evening and weekend care work and also observing pupils in residential schools as part of an earlier small-scale project (Cole 1981) and the visits we made during the project. On the latter, we observed pupils joining in activity programmes and we listened to pupils from Year 7 through to Year 11 in different settings telling us that the range of challenging 'things to do' outside class was a major reason they liked special school life. It was also noted that day pupils in residential schools were sometimes encouraged to stay on in the evenings to allow them to participate. Sometimes an overnight bed would be offered. That such pupils can share activities with friends they have made at the school and with staff with whom they have a good relationship are further bonuses.

Davies Jones (1986) points out that social pedagogues, in some countries, as part of their regular training learn how to offer a range of activities. It is recognised that such activities offered proficiently can:

- avoid deviance-inducing boredom;
- provide challenge which builds self-esteem;
- offer chance for relationship building.

To repeat an earlier idea, sharing the activity becomes the bridge between adult and young person which facilitates communication and may throw up opportunities for 'life-space' counselling. It also might throw up chances for non-verbal communication, the importance of which was stressed by Brendtro (1969). Sometimes it is good not to talk and there are times when it is politic for staff and pupils to circumvent problems by doing something different together rather than force conversation which might lead to adult–child conflict. Waiting for the right moment, as our interviewees stressed, is often crucial. Therapeutic intervention cannot be forced.

Finding occasional moments to talk and listen as adult and pupil share activities in the same life-space might sometimes be the best that can be achieved in terms of non-crisis counselling. The ability to sit down uninterrupted and talk for a prolonged period on a regular one-to-one basis remains a luxury in most special schools for pupils with EBD. In most cases only a massive increase in staffing, and therefore cost, could make this possible although with the growth over the last 20 years in the employment of LSAs, much improved RSW/pupil ratios and the employment of some care staff during daytime hours, times do present themselves when staff can listen and talk to children, sometimes in small group settings, but sometimes, with supportive teamwork among staff, on a one-to-one basis.

Kahan (1994) complains that such conversations as are possible can be of a superficial, humorous nature and fail to take a child's concerns seriously. This might sometimes be the case, but we gained the impression from replies to our questionnaire that staff consider it important that they carve out chances to communicate at both serious and humorous level with pupils.

Contact with pupils on our visits provided some limited evidence that the young people involved appreciated that staff did their best to listen to their views in a way which possibly had not happened in their mainstream school. For all the pressures on special school staff, given their numbers and the small groups with which they work there is more chance to talk than there is in the mainstream. Further, in residential schools RSWs also have many opportunities to get to know the children, find out about their backgrounds and discover ways to cajole and persuade.

Many opportunities for life-space talking and listening occur when children are playing without need for close supervision or even as they are watching TV. A young person and a RSW can also 'steal a quiet cup of tea together' in the kitchen and talk in relaxed manner about issues, for example which might have arisen from a phone call the child has just made home.

We also found that a few schools employ trained counsellors to visit in the evenings to offer qualified advice and that nearly every school seems able to offer support and counselling to pupils in the immediate aftermath of tantrums or fights. The value of Redl's 'emotional first aid' or 'therapeutic crisis intervention' (Redl and Wineman 1952) in the calm which often follows a violent explosion appears to be recognised by many and is commonly made possible by the involvement of members of the SMT in supporting the child's regular RSWs or teachers. The trouble which staff are willing to take over patching up the emotions of pupils in these situations is likely to contribute to the quality of the relationship between them and readers are referred to texts such as Cooper *et al.* 1994 for further guidance in this area. But it seems obvious that pupils will respect and respond well to staff who have expertise and will 'go the extra mile' on their behalf; who will stay to talk to them beyond the end of a shift, will give up their leisure times and breaks to meet their small requests . Adult controls, behavioural systems, a challenging range of things to do there must be, but these will only work where sound relationships exist.

The Underwood Committee claimed that 'the whole environment, both human and material in which the child grows is the true educative medium' (cited in Wilson and Evans 1980, p. 79). In this and the preceding two chapters we have only addressed the human contribution to the milieu. In the next chapter we move briefly to the 'material'.

Chapter 7

Physical Provision

The buildings themselves can have a psychological significance.
(Wilson and Evans 1980, p. 190)

'We shape our buildings – and they shape us' (attributed to Winston Churchill). (Maier 1981, p. 40)

How staff, within the constraints of site, time and money, mould the physical environment can assist or obstruct pupils' emotional well-being and therefore their availability to pursue instrumental goals. The physical environment can also hinder or help staff's delivery of the curriculum.

Research evidence shows that behaviour responds to and can be shaped by the physical environment (Moos 1974, Argyle 1978, Anderson and King 1994). Colour, light, form and space can be used positively to induce mood change and pro-social actions. Even sound in the guise of 'mood music' or Mozart (Smith 1996) wafting gently through schools is claimed to soothe 'uptight' pupils and staff. Conversely, the physical environment can precipitate the undesirable. Lack of personal 'territory' can induce anomie and low self-esteem while violence can increase in confined spaces; if large groups of pupils, never mind those with EBD, are compressed into cramped spaces, whether classrooms, corridors, or dinner-queues, there tend to be problems for staff. There can also be long-term effects on the pupils. Physical layout – nooks and crannies of large sites which are difficult to supervise – can facilitate bullying. Dingy classroom décor and dilapidated plant may encourage lack of respect for property. Echoing corridors and bare-boarded rooms can precipitate a crescendo of shouting and argument which become ingrained behaviour patterns. The importance of the material environment has been recognised by government and local government inspectors (DES 1989a, b, OFSTED 1995d).

We do not believe that a coat of paint or the mellifluous sounds of swirling seas will transform the ethos of a school for, as Galloway and Goodwin (1987) make clear, 'school climate will not be changed by buying a few pot plants' (p. 137). Nor is it necessary for most children with EBD for staff to go to the lengths and expense of staff at Peper Harow in covering walls with textiles or agonising over choice of colour for the toilets or individual pieces of furniture to create a physical environment which gives 'pleasure-giving sensual experiences' (Rose 1990, p. 86). But we do consider it important to create and maintain pleasant, attractive, homely and well equipped environments which allow for the six key welfare areas identified by social services inspectors (Morgan 1993): privacy, dignity, independence, choice, rights and fulfilment. This is a list with which OFSTED inspectors seem to agree in that their comments under section 6.2 of the inspection framework are sometimes based on a wide interpretation of the injunction to report 'on the extent to which . . . the accommodation allows the curriculum to be taught effectively' (OFSTED 1995d, p. 114).

An attractive physical environment, which meets quantitative and qualitative criteria, is a sign of a caring school which recognises the importance of allowing for pupils' physiological and affective needs. Kahan (1994) argued in relation to child care that it shows the children that they are worthy of adult respect and attention. Parents and carers can be reassured that their children are being properly looked after (Wilson and Evans 1980). Also, the weight of inspectorial evidence – both HMI, RgI and social services – points to a pleasant physical environment making the job of staff so much easier; they have more chance of delivering the many facets of the National Curriculum and a care environment which builds pupil self-concept and allows 'self-actualisation'. Redl and Wineman's (1957, p. 6) plea for 'a home that smiles, props which invite, space which allows' remains a haunting evocation of what is required and applies as much to the day as the residential settings for pupils with EBD. Indeed, many mainstream schools evoke these epithets and in doing so meet some of the needs of their pupils with EBD.

Physical provision must allow for individual pupil space, group living, whole community gatherings and physical activity (e.g. gymnasia and space for running around) permitting the pursuit of the full range of educational and care goals. It must allow for the affective, the cognitive and the psychomotor development of the pupils.

This is not always easy to achieve and managers have at varying times conflicting demands placed upon them:

- *Allowing for privacy v. facilitating adult control and supervision.* A topical example is the extent to which it is ethical to 'bug' pupils' conversations or to monitor pupil behaviour in their leisure time by close circuit television (Caring for Children 1996). This might well

133

be sensible in community and circulation areas but should pupil bedrooms be 'baby-alarmed'?

- *Locked doors v. freedom of access and development of trust and independence.* Light-fingered children cause serious upset for peers and staff – and also for children's parents when suddenly a valuable Christmas present disappears from a pupil's bedside locker. The hole knocked in the wall of the attractive new care unit can cause access to pupils' bedrooms to be denied at lunch times. If staff are not available to supervise this area, the decision may be taken to keep the unit locked.

- *Creating a warm, homely environment v. health and safety regulations.* Not long ago the school kitchen could be the emotional home of many children (Lennhoff 1968) – a natural place for counselling, near the Aga over a shared cup of coffee, round an old wooden table; now 'germ-laden pupils' are banned and all fixtures are of stainless steel. Equally schools have had to install more 'EBD inducing' fire-doors with the result that many parts of buildings can no longer be used for valued, long-established practices.

- *Lack of resources v. need to repair damage quickly.* Bettelheim (1950, p. viii) wrote 'anything broken has to be fixed as soon as possible, because it is an invitation to more breakage'. This was the philosophy of many of the headteachers we interviewed, but where is the necessary money and availability of labour to come from? One new headteacher said to his pupils: 'Cut the repair bill for deliberate damage and I will buy you the drinks machine you have been asking me for.' Vandalism decreased and the drinks machine was observed in situ by the authors.

The components of an appropriate physical environment are omitted from Circular 9/94 (DfE 1994b) and OFSTED (1995d) but are covered by the recently updated Schools Premises Regulations (DfEE 1996). The latter develops earlier government publications, notably DES (1965) and DHSS (1970) and provides a framework which is compatible with residential social work theory old and new (e.g. Bettelheim 1950, Dockar-Drysdale 1968, Maier 1981, Morgan 1993, Kahan 1994).

Many desirable features were observed by the authors on their visits to 'good practice' schools. OFSTED reports also describe well maintained, comfortable and graffiti-free environments. Social service inspection reports go into much greater detail for residential schools, sometimes praising the accommodation offered. Some key components of the desired physical environment are described below, starting with the needs of the individual child and moving outwards through provision for groups to provision for the whole school community.

Indoor provision

DfEE (1996) talks of two basic design approaches to boarding provision, which derive from the 'block' or 'cottage' style institutions of earlier generations (Cole 1986).

1. The 'family model' is characterised by children sleeping in small bedrooms containing between one and four children. They will also be a part of a group (we shall call it 'a care unit') of between eight and 20 housed in a semi-detached or detached building, usually physically separate from the teaching areas. Each care unit could be a mixed community with a wide age-span.
2. The 'communal living model' where typically larger dormitories exist and children are divided into same-age groupings of 10 to 15 perhaps as part of larger houses (in schools for pupils without SEN) of up to 60 pupils.

They also note various 'hybrid' arrangements. At times of the day (lessons or part of the evenings) different care units or houses might combine to use the wider facilities of the school. Whatever the model or 'hybrid' variation there will be provision for the following.

Comfortable and comforting individual territory

Maier (1981, p. 37) stressed that 'bodily comfort speaketh the loudest' and also discussed the difficulties of providing privacy in the 'fish bowl of group living' (p. 43). Balbernie (1966) alluded to the belief of the 1946 Curtis Report on Children's Homes: the best allowed the young people to personalise their bedrooms and to keep their own treasures and mementoes. DfEE (1996) takes these messages to heart, particularly in relation to children 'fighting demons within' as well as those struggling to rub along with the rest of the world. In this DfEE seems to have taken on board the views of pupils with EBD attending residential special schools gathered as part of Morgan's (1993) work for the Department of Health. To accompany a somewhat idyllic line drawing of a child peacefully reading on a comfortable bed, is the text:

> The ideal arrangement, whether in a single room or a bed space in a shared room, is a rectangular space in proportion not far off a square.

This should contain a bed, a bedside cabinet, a chair and clothes storage, both hanging and on shelves or in drawers. There should be shelves for books and other personal belongings, pinboard, a mirror and an adjustable light or lights for the work surface and to allow for reading in bed. There should also be some lockable storage for private personal belongings . . . where a room is shared with more than one other person, the furnishing should identify private territory associated with each personal space and provide a degree of privacy to each sleeping area. (DfEE 1996, p. 15)

When Heads of Care think of the cost of buying angle-poise lamps or the problems which lost keys and broken locks can cause, the DfEE sketch remains more a goal to which to strive than the bottom-line to satisfy inspectors. In the course of our visits, some very homely bedrooms and larger dormitories containing highly personalised and pleasant individual bed-spaces were observed. There were many more where clearly an effort had been made to create a non-institutional environment. If a policy of repairing damage quickly is pursued, it does seem possible to maintain pleasant bedrooms which pupils can enjoy and increasingly respect. They become more than a place to sleep. They become a refuge and their personal territory to which they may be allowed access at any time outside lessons (subject to site design and the practicalities of supervision) as Beedell (1970) advised.

We saw single bedrooms, double bedrooms and skilfully divided larger dormitories. DfEE advises against low-level partitions and we did not see many. It warns that, even where these exist, beds must still be 0.9 m apart (three foot) – a long-standing regulation which is not always observed. Indeed, we also observed over-crowded dormitories where the regulation metreage per bed as laid down in SI 909 (see Cole 1986, p. 101) had apparently been ignored. The room areas now suggested in DfEE (1996) are more generous but arguably unrealistic – between 7.5 sq. m and 11 sq. m for older pupils. Repeating the message of Morgan (1993), bunks for older pupils were not advised, while 'cabin beds' (of medium height with drawers and cupboards for storage underneath) did find favour. On our visits we saw few of the former.

We did note the practice of residential schools attaching day pupils to care units so that they too could make a claim to 'territory' which they might see as their own. For pupils in day schools, too often this was no more than a corner of a locker-room or their desk in their 'home-base' classroom. Moving from room to room from specialist teacher to specialist teacher should not stop the provision of some personal and small group space for day pupils.

'Un-institutional' washrooms and sanitary provision

Washing facilities and toilets should be well maintained, regularly cleaned, within easy reach of bedrooms and preferably in small domestic style bathrooms rather than in one large central block. Toilets, baths and showers must also allow for privacy and social service inspectors rightly check that locks are in place on toilet doors. Toilets for daytime use should similarly be well maintained and regularly supervised.

Comfortable lounges and group living areas

In both 'family' and 'communal living' models there should be comfortable rooms for recreation capable of accommodating all members of the care unit and their duty staff. Our observations suggest that a high standard of comfort and 'domestication' is achieved and maintained in these rooms. Whittaker (1979) noted the physical comfort of American residential centres but complained: 'There is often a sterility of atmosphere reminiscent of airport waiting rooms, an absence of art and artefacts and a peculiar unlived in feeling' (p. 87). We commonly observed personalised lounges with a 'lived in' air where staff and pupils had gone shopping together for second-hand furniture as part of life-skills training and ended up creating pleasant rooms adorned with meaningful knick-knacks and models which the young people viewed as 'theirs' – particularly, as was observed more than once, if some of their number and their care and teaching staff, had assisted with the decorations. Of course the practicalities of spilled paint, lack of skills and time-constraints make this a difficult but not impossible venture – particularly for KS4 pupils as part of design technology or vocational training programmes as advised by Wilson and Evans (1980).

Not to be forgotten were the lounges provided occasionally in day schools for senior year groups, although financial constraints meant that it was rare for funding to have been sufficient to furnish these attractively. In some day schools, where offices had had to be carved out of recesses in corridors and there was scarcely enough classroom accommodation, such provision was clearly an unobtainable luxury. In these, the classroom enhanced with a few comfortable chairs and a piece of carpet, was the only comfortable area available for recreation and for group discussions and life-space counselling.

Sound-proofed circulation areas

The headteacher of a 'recovered' school described how one of his early acts had been to carpet a barn-like corridor and to lower a high ceiling in a recently built classroom block. We watched as the school transferred in quiet and orderly fashion from class to class as the headteacher sketched the noisy chaos which the old design had exacerbated. The high ceilings and long dingy corridors of 'country house' schools can often benefit from similar upgrading.

Pleasant eating areas

We observed various attractive and contrasting environments for eating from large panelled rooms in the homes of the former aristocracy to rooms of more domestic scale in 'family style' schools. Often the acoustics had been aided by soft furnishings and curtains but one of the most orderly meals observed took place in a primary school which in mainstream fashion used the gym. In this school, virtually every member of staff sat with the children throughout the meal, helping to make it a therapeutic occasion which could be used for social skills development.

It was also common in larger schools, where the community uses central facilities for set meals, for there to be small kitchenettes and areas for eating on the care units. These were a useful adjunct for evening and perhaps early morning 'life-skills' work with pupils preparing snacks, supper or breakfast. Health and safety considerations must of course remain to the fore.

Well-appointed classrooms

Opinion remains divided over whether in residential establishments 'school' should be provided in physically separate accommodation from 'home'. Wills (1971) advocated this while DHSS (1970) claimed that 'where there is no longer a sharp distinction between school and home, children find it easier to accept an educational programme' (p. 55). Our respondents revealed that the debate continued and was sometimes reflected in the architecture of the schools. There seems to be a trend towards providing new, more homely, small-roomed care accommodation which often places physical distance between 'home' and 'school' but it was not clear whether this is just architectural expedience necessitated by planning considerations or a conscious choice of senior staff driven by their beliefs.

The OFSTED (1995d, p. 115) inspection framework notes that 'there are no statutory standards for assessing the adequacy of teaching accommodation' but that DfEE bulletins give guidance. Certainly School Premises Regulations (SPRs) in the past have specified age-related areas which should be provided per child in class which independent schools found hard to ignore if they wished to obtain and keep approved status. However, we observed education being delivered in a range of rooms of style and size.

Comment on the special school classroom also appertains to mainstream classrooms in terms of brightness and resources, and work on walls showing pupil achievement and, it is hoped, boosting pupil self-image. Perhaps, the small class numbers on the special school roll, allowing smaller more intimate rooms, make the achievement of pleasant learning environments easier to achieve subject, of course, to funding. Additional space per pupil is often an advantage, while carpets and soft furnishings can contribute to quiet, comfortable and purposeful areas for non-messy subjects. Careful attention to the arrangement of furniture to cater for individual needs and for the kind of activity will come as second nature to the skilled teacher. In our visits we observed seating at individual desks with clear gangways between rows being used to good effect by one teacher for a language lesson, while in other classes pupils sat beside each other, two to a table. Group work seated around tables with pupils' backs to the teacher may not be as productive for pupils with EBD as for 'ordinary' children. We also listened to a technology teacher's argument in favour of rearranging the work benches in his room so that each child faced towards walls rather than towards each other. Further, he was dividing the area where they sat at tables for design work from the space where the practical work took place.

Arguably, proficient schools will require sufficient rooms to allow for the delivery of specialist subjects, although RgI would seem to have differing views on whether a science room is essential or whether mobile science trolleys, particularly for KS1 and 2, will suffice. They will also need facilities for technology, both food and resistant materials, and modern computer hardware probably in a separate IT classroom but also spread through the different classrooms and perhaps evening care units. The value of computers to motivate in education and recreation was widely recognised in the schools we visited.

Quiet rooms

DfEE (1996, p. 40) says that in schools for pupils with EBD providing 'suitable spaces for counselling is particularly important'. In practice we observed counselling happening in a variety of settings – corridors, lobbies, staff offices, care unit lounges and sometimes in the quaintly named 'quiet rooms'. This term seemed to be preferred to 'time-out' rooms, although this was often their function and pupils were observed being taken unceremoniously to these rooms. One, in a recently built classroom block had no window but did have a carpet and a beanbag. Another had a window but also a large mirror; the headteacher argued that when the children saw themselves 'acting out' in violent or bizarre fashion it came as a shock and not something of which they were proud and that this calmed them down and speeded the 'recovery' process. In one school we saw a small cottage in the grounds devoted to counselling and 'time out'. This was always staffed by a duty RSW who would carry out administration tasks while awaiting 'clients'.

Adequate halls, gymnasia

Proficient schools will arguably also need large rooms for gatherings of the whole community. Assemblies in newer schools are commonly held in the gymnasium, a useful asset in any school, but some 'country house' schools have to travel to local sports centres to gain access to a covered sufficiently expansive area for team games. In old buildings there may well exist attractive oak-panelled former drawing rooms which lend themselves to indoor games as well as formal gatherings, sometimes adapting better to the needs of the present than the purpose-built rooms created in the 1960s and 1970s when views on the size of schools (see below) were rather different.

Sufficient staff rooms

It seems to be generally agreed that an office for the members of SMTs who are directly responsible for the delivery of the education programmes, or acting in the 'crisis teacher' role, should be at the heart of the classroom provision – certainly in schools which are fortunate to have these in one block. The headteacher of one school talked of 'the umbrella effect' of having his deputy's office in a central position, and next door to the 'quiet room'. He praised the teaching abilities of a teacher opposite but feared that without the presence of the deputy nearby, who was known as an effective 'disciplinarian', the teacher's control and the quality of the pupils' work may have suffered. Indeed, to aid his view of the main corridors, an additional internal window was being installed with views along the corridors. From the other side of this suite of rooms was an uninterrupted view of the playgrounds and fields, aiding break time supervision. These rooms can be, and are, used by the headteacher but at other times he felt he needed to retreat from the 'front-line' to his own room where he knows he can talk in comfort and peace to visitors, parents or devote time to administration or strategic planning.

Another practice which we observed was placing the Head of Care's room or the general staff room for RSWs at the heart of the classrooms, helping them to be accessible to children during daytime hours when they were on duty and facilitating communications between them and teachers. These rooms were in addition to facilities for RSWs, by way of small offices and/or 'sleeping in' rooms on the care units.

Most schools also have general staff rooms, which might sometimes be shared with cleaning, maintenance and other support staff as well as teaching and care staff. In these, the pupils' presence was generally not encouraged to allow for necessary adult recuperation. If SPRs are followed, there will also be shower facilities and washrooms, necessary for that speedy change at the end of afternoon PE lessons as the staff member gets ready for an evening care duty. Of course many establishments, usually day schools, are not blessed with space. One 'good practice' school had only one room for use as a reception room for visitors, the headteacher's office and the general staff room.

Visitors' rooms

If work with parents, especially family therapy, is to be a reality, it is necessary to have rooms which can be devoted to this purpose. These should be areas to which parent and child or parent and staff can retreat away from the hurly-burly of normal school life. They have been known to take the shape of a caravan in the grounds or in a few independent schools, following Danish and American practice, specially built bungalows on the peaceful fringes of the school site. When not being used by parents, these become useful adjuncts for consultants, visiting professionals or students. For day schools on cramped urban sites these are likely to remain a distant dream.

Outdoor provision

We observed the shrinking playing field of one urban school, sacrificed for a profitable new housing estate, but this school remained better endowed with space than many described by HMI in the 1980s (DES 1989b). There remained adequate tarmac areas as well as grassed playing field on which we watched pupils running and playing at lunch time but generally sites on the edge of town or in rural locations have distinct advantages in terms of outside space. On our visits to the latter we saw carefully crafted adventure playgrounds which were easily observed by staff from within the care units and classrooms, and extensive lawns and woods in country house schools. In addition, many had football pitches and we saw much imaginative use of open spaces including the provision of a go-kart track. Sometimes, though, sites were too large and there were supervision problems at lunch times and in the care hours – echoed by comments in OFSTED reports about opportunities for bullying. On the other hand they allowed a degree of freedom unavailable to children on cramped urban sites. The space permitted discreetly supervised adventure games in which scope could be given for pupils to exercise their imaginations. It also allowed rough and tumble play, seen as a natural part of childhood development by Blatchford and Sharp (1994). Play is:

> what children do . . . a practice of skills, an experiment toward adult life, an exploration of the environment, a bridge to areas of thought and feeling outside the self. (Myerscough in Lennhoff 1968, p. B19).

Where there are extensive grounds, some of them (especially the parts which visitors see) should be well kept but other areas can be allowed to be unkempt and open to younger pupils to use for imaginative play. Flower beds which are pristine and neatly trimmed edges to lawns can suggest regimes which devote too much attention to appearances and perhaps over-supervise and over-organise their pupils.

We also observed the existence of school minibuses in most schools, which ranged from new vehicles to creaking old warhorses. One headteacher had boldly painted out the stigmatising Variety Club label. For day schools school vehicles might be useful adjuncts of life. For residential schools, they are essential for transporting children to and from home and for the wide range of educational and recreational activities so valued by the pupils to whom we talked and the pupils attending residential special schools interviewed by Morgan (1993). The canoe trailer is another useful appendage and likely to be much used in many schools.

The optimal site for an EBD school

Does the proficient school for pupils with EBD need to be surrounded, as Wills (1971) suggested for the Cotswold Community, by a 'cordon sanitaire' (p. 105) of acres of farmland? Many, of course, are. LEAs and private organisations followed government advice in the wake of the 1944 Education Act and turned the former mansions of prime ministers, field marshals and impecunious gentry into schools during the 'country house period' (Ministry of Education 1956). It was a noticeable feature of our visits that nearly every 'good practice' school possessed ample space, some of it green and natural, dividing the site from village or small town. This facilitated the range of outdoor play and organised physical activities described above.

At the edge of these sites there was sometimes a tall fence – not to keep the pupils in (an unnecessary act as our data show the very rare occurrence of absconding from our sample schools) – but rather, we were told, to deter the unwanted attentions of the youths of the neighbourhood whose behaviour could be more EBD than that of the pupils. The spiked steel barriers surrounding town schools serve a similar purpose but probably proving their worth more frequently. Time has not permitted a detailed study of the sites of EBD schools to check out whether there is a correlation between cramped city sites set in areas of socio-economic difficulty and OFSTED verdicts of 'serious weaknesses' and 'special measures' or whether cramped urban sites might be linked with 'poor' standards. However, we did make an assessment of 86 OFSTED reports. Of the 40 best reports, the vast majority referred to country or small town schools offering residential accommodation. It should be noted that many of these schools admitted pupils from difficult inner city areas. It therefore seems reasonable to hypothesise that siting schools on the fringes of small towns or in the countryside might facilitate the modelling of different behaviours and expectancies which can assist in addressing pupils' emotional and behavioural difficulties. This might be better practice, rather than pursuing a utopian notion of 'community based provision'.

Is there an optimal size?

The Underwood Committee (Ministry of Education 1955) recommended schools with between 20 and 50 pupils. DHSS (1970) for the new Community Homes with Education (CHEs) suggested no more than 60 pupils, smaller than some of the old Home Office approved schools. As reported in Chapter 2, both Dawson (1980) and the present authors found average numbers in the forties.

However, we did see an impressive small school with only 24 pupils, but with a good and committed staff and in a pleasant situation which elicited an excellent response from its pupils. OFSTED inspectors gave a very favourable report on a school with only six pupils. Conversely they also praised a school with over 90 pupils and one with 70 pupils which wanted to extend its provision by a further 16. These were schools we visited and we were similarly impressed by so much of what we saw.

There is clearly potential for economy and efficiency in greater numbers. Per capita costs are lower and it is easier to employ a wide range of subject specialists to cover all areas of the National Curriculum as well as to facilitate the provision of outdoor pursuits, bricklaying, decorating and other training or recreational activities.

But what of the difficulties of management which might increase in intensity and complexity as size increases? Is it possible still to achieve unity of values and practice amongst staff; to keep teaching and care standards high? Can the quality of relationships and the 'family model' work in larger schools? Can an overall therapeutic ethos be engendered as easily? In response to these and other questions we were told by headteachers of the large schools we visited that problems of size could be overcome by good organisation, the employment of the right staff and the availability of suitable teaching and care accommodation.

In general, when we asked the senior staff of 'good practice' schools their views on optimal size, they tended to give their present number of pupils on roll. All the above factors considered, we would not contest government advice (DfE 1994b) that as a general guide the size of the school should not prevent the delivery of the National Curriculum. For residential schools, the wide range of active social pedagogy described in Chapter 6 also indicates the benefits of larger staff groups in relation to the school's ability to offer a wide range of worthwhile activities. Our personal preference taking into consideration curriculum, ethos and financial considerations if planning a school from scratch, would be for about 60 pupils.

Conclusion

While the human contribution to the proficient school is of primary importance, careful attention paid to physical design, maintenance and development, which in practice, as Maier (1981) acknowledged, usually means making the best of the buildings, the site and the location which have been given to you, does make a significant contribution to the achievement of effectiveness. The physical and material cannot be left out of the model of overall proficiency which we describe in the final chapter.

Chapter 8

Effective Schooling for Pupils with Emotional and Behavioural Difficulties

This final chapter draws together the elements which we have identified as characterising proficient special school provision for pupils with EBD but many have universality and could be applied in any setting containing pupils labelled as EBD. Thus, we believe that if they were replicated to a greater extent in mainstream environments there would be less need to exclude and segregate so many pupils. Many pupils with EBD can, and do, have their needs met in mainstream schools. However, world-wide experience suggests that there will always remain a need for alternative provision. Some pupils, no matter how good the mainstream 'offer', clearly benefit from a fresh start in smaller schools, where better staff/pupil ratios facilitate the formation of stable, positive relationships between skilful and committed adults and children and where that vital ingredient, time, can more easily be found for individual attention to be given to pupils' affective and cognitive needs. Wider, social factors also indicate a continuing need for some residential provision as the recent government 'green paper' recognises (DfEE 1997).

In Chapter 1 we noted that the word 'proficient' meant 'expert and adept in doing'. However, while it signifies 'expertness', it does not imply absolute perfection. This reflects the word's derivation from the Latin verb '*proficere*' which means 'to make progress'. It, thus, neatly encapsulates both effectiveness and the concern of many writers (e.g. Stoll and Fink 1994) for exploring not only the factors which characterise the effective school, but also the processes associated with school improvement.

The term proficient also reflects the dynamic quality and realism of the 'good practice' schools which we visited. These schools did not rest on their laurels. Senior staff saw a continuing need for improvement in a range of areas, often identified with staff and made public through their school development plans. These are schools where learning did not end and where an awareness of their mission guided staffs' choice of objectives and prioritisation of goals in relation to all the key variables of their provision (see next section). Similarly, implementation of policy was subject to ongoing review and this led, in turn, to greater understanding and learning which was used to adjust future objectives and the methods employed to realise them. Following the clear but responsive direction of the headteacher and SMT, staff 'do', then 'review', then 'learn' and finally 'apply' the lessons learnt in a continuous cycle which gave these schools forward momentum.

Key variables in proficient provision

According to our findings the factors associated with effectiveness which assist in the management of challenging behaviour in the mainstream (see Chapter 2) seem to apply with equal force to special schools for pupils with EBD (Cooper *et al.* 1994). This is apparent in Table 8.1 which highlights the four dimensions, which preceding chapters have addressed, *population, people, provision* and *place*. The nature of the pupils, and to a lesser extent their parents, who make up the *population* do have an important bearing on outcomes and processes but it seems to be the people who work with them, their personalities and what they plan and do, that matter most. Schools seem most effective when committed staff of the right calibre come together under effective leadership and good relationships exist between the headteacher and the governors, LEA or independent owners who give the school efficient professional support.

But policies appear equally crucial for the provision of appropriate and well organised *programmes* which challenge and engage the pupils. The proficient school seems able to set 'normal' goals, such as are pursued by peers in the mainstream, which address pupils' educational needs but also address pupils' individual expressive or affective needs, in particular the need to build self-esteem. School-wide systems for behaviour management are also important, while the success of programmes seems to be dependent on the existence of warm, caring and long-lasting relationships between staff and pupils. Finally, proficiency seems significantly aided, or obstructed, by physical and material resources: the 'look and feel of a school' does impact on quality of provision and size and physical location also has a bearing.

Table 8.1 The proficient school for pupils with emotional and behavioural difficulties

---

Proficiency is the product of

Population
- **pupils**
  - sufficient in number to permit a broad curriculum and same–age peer groups
  - SMT have some control over who attends their school

- **parents**
  - support won and sustained by the school staff

People
- **pedagogues**
  - well led by an energetic headteacher who is supported by able SMT
  - skilled, experienced, committed teachers, RSWs, etc. with sympathy for EBD

- **professional support**
  - school is adequately resourced and supported by LEA, health services, etc.

Provision
- **policies**
  - comprehensive policies on education, behaviour and care put into effect and regularly reviewed

- **programmes**
  - differentiated IEPs and care plans, paying attention to the affective. Building self-esteem through achievement and leading to 'normal' goals

Place
- **physical plant**
  - the home that smiles, props which invite, space which allows catering for individual, group and community needs
  - in touch with local community
  - efficient transport links with homes

Population

Pupils

There are two variables under this topic which appear to impact particularly heavily on proficiency. One is quantitative, namely the size of a school; the other, is qualitative, the nature of a school's pupil population.

One OFSTED report we examined praised a school containing a mere handful of pupils; while we observed a pleasant and successful school containing only three classes of eight pupils. Small schools with good staff can clearly work well in many respects and might be the best practical solution in particular parts of the country. However, as a general rule our findings support the contention (DfE 1994b) that there should be sufficient numbers on roll to allow the employment of a range of staff who can offer a broad and balanced curriculum and in the case of residential schools quality care beyond the meeting of 'lower level' needs. Bigger schools can also facilitate the formation of same, or similar, aged peer groups although in residential schools children need to live in small, homely units to allow for personalised care.

We accept the contention of most of the respondents to our questionnaire that care needs to be taken to ensure that pupils' behaviour is not of excessively violent or criminal nature as this can make the achievement of a positive ethos impossible. Forcing a plethora of confirmed delinquents or repeatedly violent, sexual or drug abusing pupils into schools for pupils with EBD is not good practice, even if 'there is nowhere else for them to go'. Nor should the severely psychotic who require intensive psychiatric involvement be placed there. This treatment cannot be provided in most schools for pupils with EBD.

Proficient special schools for pupils with EBD appear able to admit, contain and motivate some very challenging children. Usually a combination of generous staff/pupil ratios; staff expertise, determination and resilience; school systems and availability of staff time assist pupils in settling into them. At times pupils present extreme challenges to staff but proficient schools seem to battle through. They are usually extremely reluctant to exclude pupils being aware that their pupils have experienced too much rejection in their lives already. However, there are limits and it is important that LEAs listen when a special school, respected for its ability and competence, says a child is beyond its control or may seriously damage other pupils physically or morally. Even in the very best schools there are occasions when the long-term good of the school community has to come before the shorter-term needs of a particular child. The lesson from our study of proficient schools and 'recovering' schools is that transfers planned in conjunction with the pupil, family and professionals are desirable. These seem more effective than reliance on exclusion of pupils although occasionally this is necessary. We remain suspicious of establishments which told us that they admit any child and operate a 'non-exclusions' policy. These are admirable theoretical positions, often reflecting the kinds of personal values which must be held by SMTs, but taking such high moral ground might lead to other children, as well as staff, suffering in a way which is not in anyone's long-term interests.

Evidence from our study also suggests that some control by SMTs over who is admitted to a school is important for the well-being of staff in helping shake off the negative image of special schools for pupils with EBD which makes it so difficult to attract skilled mainstream practitioners. More importantly though, it makes it easier to achieve, sustain and develop a positive ethos when the school is not under prolonged violent attack from a minority who persistently fail to respond to staff approaches. Leadership will be diverted from the plethora of duties outlined in Chapter 5. Much 'fire-fighting' there will always be, but SMTs should not be overwhelmed by multiple conflagrations which they cannot realistically extinguish.

Parents

It was a consistent message from our respondents that the support of parents or substitute carers must be won and sustained and a model of proficiency must therefore allow for work with the family. This is an old idea:

> While children are in attendance at the School, their homes are visited with a view to ensuring the co-operation of the parents which in the majority of cases is regularly given. (*City of Leicester Annual Report 1932*, cited in Bridgeland 1971, p. 299)

In line with the precedent set by this early Leicester initiative, schools should do whatever is within their often limited means to win and maintain the support of a child's family. According to our evidence this decreasingly means (unless there are suspicions of child abuse) working through the services offered by overworked local authority field social work departments. If the calls for closer inter-agency working, made for generations (Cole 1989) and repeated in the OFSTED framework (1995d) and in the 1997 'green paper' (DfEE 1997), do bear fruit, the delivery of practical family support and therapy by skilled health or social service personnel which concentrate on altering ways parent and child with EBD relate to one another (Chazan *et al.* 1994; Asen 1996), would seem a priority. Of course such a policy has expensive resource, and difficult organisational, implications.

In the meantime, the 'good letters' home, home–school diaries, regular phone calls and a twice-termly visit mentioned by our respondents, while not substitutes for sustained family support, seem to be appreciated by parents and help relationship building even though they may only scratch the surface of many deep-seated family difficulties. Enabling teachers and other staff to spend time on family work as well as delivering a broad, balanced and differentiated National Curriculum or quality care is not easy, yet this is expected in the OFSTED inspection framework in which space is devoted to the theme of parents as partners and most proficient schools do manage productive work in this area.

People

Leadership

A keystone of proficient provision seems to be the quality of leadership provided by the SMT and in particular by the headteacher. Charlton and David (1993) among others suggest that a consultative, cooperative style of leadership which allows staff to develop ideas within an overall set of parameters set by the headteacher, makes for proficient provision (see also Cole and Visser 1998). In such an environment a sense of loyalty and willingness to agree with requests seems to be evoked from staff and parents who appreciate that these headteachers will 'go the extra half mile' with them and, most importantly, with the pupils. This form of leadership seems to build up 'banks of goodwill' which see schools through the periods of emotional turmoil which typify work with these pupils.

But this subtle, personable and usually 'up front' leadership style does not come easily. Our discussions with headteachers suggest that many had seen a need in the initial phase of their headship to be autocratic. Few of the headteachers of the schools that we visited took over schools which were running smoothly or could be said to be proficient. Indeed it was common for headteachers in our survey to have taken over schools which had been seen by either OFSTED or the LEA as having serious weaknesses. Strong directive leadership appears necessary in these situations before a more open style can be adopted. But where strong leadership is provided, it seems possible to turn round apathetic or defeatist staff attitudes within relatively short periods.

Long-term proficiency appears difficult to attain and maintain unless the headteacher is supported by an able deputy. The burden is too great and the tasks too diverse for one person. In a residential school, a committed and competent Head of Care is also needed but this triumvirate must have a clear view of the school they want and a good understanding of the complexities of pupils with EBD and their families. Our study found senior staff in our 'good practice' schools to be very committed as individuals and as teams. They were experienced and very skilled in working with pupils and parents. They had 'bi-focal' vision, clearly seeing what was happening close to them while also focusing on where the school was in relation to the local community and the wider world. For example, while well aware of national regulations and standards of achievement, they set rules and horizons which met the individual needs of pupils in their schools. Key to this appeared to be the ability of senior managers to communicate what was happening, why it was happening and what it was intended to achieve to the pupils, staff, parents and governors within the school and to LEA officers, health and social services and the community.

It also seems important that SMTs have time and energy to devote to the four aspects of staff management mentioned in Chapter 5: selection; induction; monitoring and development – and maintenance of the 'E factor'. We have stressed already that it is the people in a school who are central to achieving effectiveness but there are problems to address even with the most skilled and well motivated staff. Keen new staff need guidance; experienced staff become stale, they fail to notice their own incipient bad habits, they become tired, they become ill. A 'horticultural' approach, which tends and feeds, grows and supports has been commended earlier as beneficial for adults and pupils. Staff development is a never-ending task. Caring for staff, when the going gets tough, through careful supervision, is also an important aspect of the long-term proficient school.

Staff: teachers, RSWs and support staff

Proficiency cannot be provided 'on the cheap'. Staff ratios govern the degree of individual attention and the time for programme planning which is essential if proficiency is to be achieved. As we have indicated in

Chapter 4, Circular 11/90 (DES 1990) remains a desirable but often unachievable guide to good practice, particularly in the area of learning support assistants. For teaching and care staff it is essential that schools do not fall too far short of the advised ratios but quantity of staffing is not the sole answer. It is the quality of staff, particularly their commitment and motivation which plays an important part in achieving proficiency. Other personality traits have been described in some detail in Chapter 4. On our evidence, proficient teachers seem, by habit, to be good planners and organisers; are consistent and fair; can laugh with (not at) the children; have an empathy for children with difficulties; have even, determined temperaments and many other personal qualities which also tend to characterise good RSWs and other school staff. Behind an outward confidence, they also possess a certain humility and are willing to listen, both to children and their parents but also to their colleagues.

Thus, the key players – teachers, RSWs and LSAs , not just SMTs – in the proficient schools we saw did not think that they 'knew it all' or that they had 'got things right'. But they believed in their abilities, those of their colleagues and their systems. This contributed to an essential 'can-do' culture. Yet they were happy subscribing to the 'learning school' philosophy in which a dynamic 'do-review-learn-apply' cycle informed all aspects of school life. They also seemed to talk a lot informally, but also in more formal meetings, about their work and these discussions went beyond letting off steam about the difficulties of the children or staff's conditions of service and looked for practical solutions to problems. Debate seeks to improve personal practice and the operation of school systems especially if staff are encouraged by SMTs to contribute to revisions of school policies.

Support for the school from outside agencies

Unfortunately, there are LEAs whose policy on EBD has been in a chronic state of flux for a long time. In one authority, acting headteachers of special schools have held temporary positions for years. Such a lack of support might be a factor explaining why so many schools have fared badly in OFSTED inspections. We were also struck by the number of respondents saying that their LEA was undertaking another review of EBD provision. Sometimes this was because of local government reorganisation, sometimes because of financial crises and sometimes because 'inclusionist' administrators hoped to create alternatives to their special schools. Whatever the cause of the uncertainty, it was hardly conducive to nurturing better practice in these Authorities' schools. SMTs must have reliable practical and moral support from their LEAs, or in the case of independent schools, from their owners. Proficient schools seem to be characterised by close working relationships between the headteacher and the school governors.

Similarly, well-established and mutually trusting relationships with educational psychologists, education welfare officers and other 'outside' professionals seems important.

Provision: policies

A hallmark of the proficiency which we saw was the comprehensive nature of written documentation covering all aspects of education and care, behaviour management and health and safety issues and other legal requirements. A further feature was the clarity of these documents. Much thought, based on a sound understanding of both theoretical, legal and practical issues, had clearly gone into writing them. While in the main they had been the work of SMTs, other staff had been involved in their construction (and regular review), helping to produce accessible working documents which were owned by the staff.

Following the advice of DfE (1994b) all schools should have thorough behaviour management policies. Policies help focus attention on individual needs but they also respond to the expectations of the wider community for consistent and fair systems, clearly understood by staff and by pupils. Where this is the case, safe, well-organised schools with staff clearly in control tend to result. Well-established routines, reward and sanction systems provide pupils with the supportive 'rubber boundaries' and education, care and behaviour policies contribute to the fostering of self-esteem, achievement and progress towards greater independence. Such systems allow time for, and encourage, staff to listen and talk to pupils and to provide 'emotional first aid'.

Provision: programme delivery

Proficient pedagogy

Our study clearly shows that good pedagogy provided by teachers, secure in their subject knowledge, well organised, matched to individual needs and based on the 'plus one principle' (see Chapter 6) does elicit good responses, lessening the tendencies of most pupils to engage in disruptive behaviour in class. Samuels (1995) talked of good teachers being in authority because they were 'an authority'. He offered this vignette of an art teacher:

> She is so determined to pursue her subject that the children are engulfed by her enthusiasm and energy which seems to overcome their anxieties. (p. 86)

Our observations and responses from the questionnaire confirm Samuels' view. The evidence shows that children who have caused chaos in other settings often behave well in special classes and schools once suitably differentiated and skilled teaching is offered. Their previous disruption often appears to have been a response to imperfect environments (Burt and Howard 1952 cited in Bridgeland 1971, Galloway 1990, DfE 1994a and b).

Our respondents suggested that when new pupils arrive, they are likely to be suspicious and hostile but once they see what other pupils do in class they generally come to appreciate that teachers genuinely wish to help them; they quickly appreciate that the teachers have 'withitness', commitment and understanding and the ability to offer methods which have appeal.

A 'normal' curriculum

In the main, pupils appear to want education to be given high priority and to receive in class that which is offered in the mainstream. Frequently there will be difficult surface behaviour to manage but this is often a misleading veneer of resistance. Deep down most pupils want to be viewed as 'normal'; this means providing the National Curriculum. The Dearing reforms brought a welcome flexibility which could be extended at Key Stage 4 to offer more practical and vocational work and 'alternative' curricula which the special education 'green paper' (DfEE 1997) apparently favours. All this helps pupil management. Stress on basic skills, again in the headlines in late 1997 (Rafferty 1997), might necessitate further change to the National Curriculum at earlier Key Stages. If this reduces the breadth of what has to be taught, then this is also likely to be welcomed by some of our respondents and it will be in line with Wilson and Evans' (1980) belief that it is better to offer a somewhat narrower curriculum well than a wide one badly.

When a balanced educational curriculum is delivered imaginatively, sensitively and appropriately, allowing for a more practical, 'hands on' approach, broken down into small steps with built-in success, most pupils in EBD schools appear to respond well. Some pupils work towards GCSEs. Others, often those severely underachieving, see these as beyond their grasp, and look for other qualifications which mirror the mainstream offer at Key Stage 4. Proficient schools offer a range of such nationally accredited courses.

Building self-esteem through successful achievement

Appropriately delivered curriculum in class and care time can contribute to the building of self-esteem. This was seen as a crucial factor by our respondents but is an old message:

> There is something every child can do well . . . and we try to find what that something is. . . . When proficiency is found the child acquires a feeling of achievement and projects this feeling towards work of which he was previously afraid. Confidence in his work dispels the child's need of gaining compensation through obtrusive and difficult behaviour, so his energy is now directed into right channels and the behaviour problem clears up. (cited in Bridgeland 1971, p. 300)

This was written not by Wilson and Evans (1980) in relation to good practice, Cooper (1993) in relation to 're-signification' nor Greenhalgh (1994) although it mirrors his writing closely, but *circa* 1937 by R. A. Dewhurst, headteacher of the first LEA day school for the maladjusted to exist in England. Our data support his views. In our 'good practice' schools, staff searched out the things that pupils can do well and offered opportunities to extend the range of children's achievement, often using subject areas from the National Curriculum as the vehicle.

Addressing all levels of the Maslow Triangle

The importance of finding the 'something' which a pupil can do well and enjoy and which can be used as a launch pad for further satisfying challenges is of central importance outside the classroom as well as in it. Proficient day, but particularly residential schools, offer a range of such experiences. Generally, somewhere on that wide menu, pupils find activities to which they respond and in which they can develop their skills and build their self-worth as learners and socially acceptable young people.

Teachers are trained to recognise and act upon this need. RSWs tend not to be. Davies Jones (1986) described the role of the social pedagogue, noting that RSWs on the continent, as part of their training, learn how to offer activities to children – a practice which could be usefully copied in this country. Residential workers, who share the 'life-space' of children for long periods each week must provide good quality primary care. Addressing physiological needs with imagination and in a way which allows for privacy and dignity and individual preference is crucial – as is making children feel safe and wanted.

Pupils need opportunities to relax and to play. Independence should be fostered but to reduce disruptive behaviour, which often springs from boredom or perhaps too much time to contemplate, an engaging activities programme is required each evening. Achievement in these activities can boost self-confidence and assist 'self-actualisation'.

Reaching and supporting 'the child within'

Proficient schools can be seen as 'listening' and 'talking' schools. Their systems allow individual members of staff to hear the voice of the pupils and to offer support through 'counselling'. Our investigation has revealed much informal, though empathic and often skilled, talking and listening to children; reflecting back and exploring feelings; generally showing an interest in the pupils' lives, rather than formal counselling offered by trained personnel. The latter would not seem to happen frequently, nor is it viewed as essential for many pupils in the schools which we observed. The former is crucial to establishing the necessary helpful relationships between staff and children.

Given the generous staff/pupil ratios and the presence of LSAs in our schools, it was not surprising that opportunities for 'counselling' did occur during lessons. Counselling also occurred at planned group meetings or in PSE lessons but opportunities for informal listening and talking were offered by teachers and other support staff in breaks and at lunch times. It was common for us on our visits to observe staff making themselves available to pupils who would sidle up in corridors, bounce unannounced into offices, linger at the lunch table after the other children had gone or sit beside staff on low garden walls at break times and talk to anyone who would lend a sympathetic ear, offer encouragement or show empathy.

Skilled teacher and social pedagogues also seem skilled in using shared activities as the bridge between the child and themselves. Doing things together was identified in our study as assisting in building trusting

156

relationships and catalysing opportunities for 'life-space interviews'. Those living with the pupils often seem to 'seize the moment' when brewing coffee, cooking, tidying a bedroom, playing pool, ice-skating or fell-walking, or just before turning out a bedroom light. In time, later usually rather than sooner, suspicious, hostile children lower their defences; they start talking; the RSW or teacher listens and a dialogue develops. This can be the best form of counselling as it is often seen as more 'normal' than planned therapy; pupils do not always want to talk at an appointed hour to an appointed person, however skilled and trained. Trieschman *et al.* (1969) stressed the importance of utilising the opportunities which can be engineered or present themselves naturally in 'the Other Twenty Three Hours.' Their message was powerfully reflected in the practice we observed in proficient schools.

Our interview and questionnaire data suggest that staff advice was sometimes shaped by non-directive, Rogerian principles but there were times when they considered it appropriate to be directive and prescriptive. Children sometimes want adults to advise them what to do, as some of our respondents stressed, and can be suspicious of staff who only ask the pupils what they, the pupils, feel or think. Often they resist adult direction, but can accept that it is necessary and in their own best interests.

Skilled staff also appear to appreciate the importance of 'therapeutic crisis intervention' (see Chapter 2). Pupils often need, and are receptive to, sympathetic counselling in the immediate aftermath of an outburst and the calm which follows the storm is a good time to offer Redl's (1966) 'emotional first aid'. Our proficient schools organised themselves so that this could be offered at any time of the day, evening or indeed night, with senior, skilled staff often available for this eventuality.

More formal counselling by qualified practitioners is necessary for a minority, particularly for those recovering from particularly traumatic events or those at the psychiatric end of the EBD spectrum. Proficient schools make this available as necessary.

While staff often feel stressed by lack of time (Dunham 1992, Rogers 1994) for attending to individual pupil's need to talk, our data suggest that they make it happen far more than occurred in the pupil's previous mainstream settings. Making time for counselling permeates much of school life in the proficient EBD school, demonstrates staff's commitment to pupils' affective needs, is appreciated by the children and contributes much to the building of positive relationships.

'The art of consciously using oneself in relationship for others . . .'

In the proficient school, the fact that staff and pupils occupy the same life-space sometimes over a period of years, whether engaging together in stimulating educational day or evening experiences or restful and comforting care or talking and listening to one another, facilitates the formation of positive relationships. Closely and routinely sharing life in a warm, supportive environment, breaks down the barriers which have previously made pupils suspicious of adults and disruptive in school. As pupils come to respect the staff and enjoy their company, they can enter into relationships with them, which are at the very heart of effective practice with pupils with EBD. Our visits underlined this and we read much in the replies to our questionnaire and in schools' documentation which would support this long-held view (e.g. Wilson and Evans 1980).

'Residential treatment is an art, the art of consciously using oneself in relationship for others and to create a healing culture' (Balbernie, Foreword to Millham *et al.* 1975, p. xvii). Successful staff, he later commented, make a 'deep personal investment'. The same comment could be made with reference to staff in any educational setting for pupils with EBD, as our evidence reported in Chapter 4 suggests. The pupils, in the course of sharing their lives with the teachers, RSWs and other workers, come to appreciate the commitment of the staff and the adults' willingness to make sacrifices on the young people's behalf. Goodwill is engendered which encourages pupils to give something back. This 'return of favours' often takes the shape of reasonable and social behaviour or commitment to their educational or care programmes.

'Points mean prizes'

In our visits to schools we observed many purposeful and peaceful classroom and care situations. Engaging, motivating and controlling pupils with EBD appears in part an art, in part a craft, but at times a science. The latter underpinned the carefully devised forms of behaviour management which existed in most of our 'good practice' schools.

In Chapter 6 we reported the importance respondents attached to school-wide systems of rewards and sanctions, owned by both staff and pupils. These school-wide systems, based on warm relationships, aided the achievement of the firm and consistent discipline which we see (echoing Wilson and Evans 1980) as one of the key processes in assisting pupils with EBD. OFSTED reports show inspectors holding similar views. It is clear to us that the children themselves prefer that teachers and RSWs establish control, even if they prefer it to be relaxed. We note Millham *et al.*'s (1975) stress on the need for staff in residential schools to impinge upon pupils' worlds and to permeate and splinter incipient delinquent subcultures (Polsky 1967). This is a timeless message and applies equally to day settings. Points and rewards systems can assist. However, they must not be allowed to dominate school life or to obstruct the flexible addressing of individual needs as Vander Ven feared (see p. 121 in Chapter 6).

Pragmatic eclecticism

The 'points mean prizes' approach contrasts starkly with the methods associated with some therapeutic and psychodynamic regimes. In the latter, allowing children to 'act out' their inner troubles, as part of the treatment process, has been preferred and even seen as essential (Ministry of Education 1955). This perspective now seems to have few adherents among staff in schools for pupils with EBD.

However in good practice schools, outward behaviourism was influenced by aspects of in-depth and psychodynamic approaches. Staff were concerned about emotions beneath the surface of behaviour; they were interested in family relationships; they thought it important to understand, to hear the pupils' perceptions, to help pupils work out their own inner turmoil. School systems in proficient schools seem to possess a high degree of flexibility and responsiveness to individual need; they are not cold and mechanistic. They allow for humanist concerns and do not prevent skilled staff adopting an empathic stance. Teachers, RSWs and LSAs try to help pupils to reframe their thinking, to alter children's perceptions of self and of the world (Ayers *et al.* 1995) and to break out of self-defeating, negative cycles. In short, a pragmatic eclecticism was observed in the schools we visited as it is apparently in OFSTED inspection reports.

'The great ego-supportive power of traditionalised routine'

Redl's (1966) belief about the value of routines commanded widespread support among our respondents (see also Wilson and Evans 1980). They stressed the achievement and maintenance of a well-ordered, secure community and structured daily timetables encompassing more than directed teaching time. Fussy or over-regimented practice was avoided but simple, well-understood routines were seen as contributing to the 'rubber boundaries' outlined in Chapters 5 and 6. Even pupils with above-average abilities with whom Samuels (1995) worked were 'afraid of the anarchy in their own lives' (p. 89).

Routines provide support and on balance reduce argument between staff and pupils. They also help to foster healthy dependence on trustworthy adults, which is a necessary first step on the road to independence (Maier 1981). As Bowlby (cited in Greenhalgh 1994) advised, children are happiest when their lives are organised as a series of short excursions from a secure base. Routines are an important part of that secure base.

Pupil involvement and ownership

Our data support Samuels' (1995) contention, as well as that of DfE (1994a and b), that developing an appropriate and increasing degree of pupil responsibility through a collaborative approach is beneficial. In proficient schools pupils feel that the systems are relevant to their needs but they have chance to discuss aspects of the routines and reward systems openly and frankly with staff, sometimes contributing to the alteration of procedures or sanctions. Similarly they are involved in planning and monitoring their education and care programme targets. This collaborative style of operating does not however equate with the democratic and self-governing experiments associated with some pioneer establishments (see Chapter 2).

Place

The physical environment is not as crucial as that provided by people, but it is important. It was clear in our visits that proficient schools can be housed on sites of contrasting age, size, style and location but they are invariably warm, inviting, well-resourced buildings which allow for individual, group and whole-school needs both in lesson time and breaks and in residential schools, in the care hours. Senior managers in proficient schools do not allow geographical location, which might be rural and remote or inner city ringed by an eight foot high security fence, to be an excuse for the development of inward looking practice, out of keeping with national standards and guidance on good education and care.

Proficient schools facilitate access to the local community and are able to maintain efficient transport links with the pupils' homes.

Transposing good practice from proficient special schools

Provision for pupils with EBD in special schools would seem likely to continue to be required (DfEE 1997); indeed new schools were opened in 1996/7. While some schools, fearing or experiencing the condemnation of OFSTED, have closed, most have carried on, clearly needed by LEAs and social service departments. The task is therefore to transpose good practice into schools with weaknesses, as is recognised by DfEE (1997). Whether the practice to be disseminated is entirely encompassed by the existing OFSTED framework (see Chapter 5) is debatable. On the basis of our evidence there seems to be a need for more attention to be given in it to the assessment of behaviour management, personal and social development and in residential schools, care arrangements. (See also Visser *et al.* in press; Cole and Visser 1998). But much of the OFSTED model is in accord with the elements of proficiency identified above and is supported by us.

Recently, DfEE has been active in disseminating good practice through workshops, new written guidance and the suggested consultancy service (DfEE 1997) whereby the headteachers of 'outstanding provision' will offer support to staff in other EBD schools. This last approach has considerable potential as long as it does not add to the workload of some of the best professionals to the detriment of their own schools. This pro-active policy is welcome.

However, more immediate steps can, and must, be taken, especially in schools said to have weaknesses. These can be initiated by the staff themselves or by their LEAs. Some can be implemented relatively cheaply and simply without too much difficulty. We were taken aback when an acting headteacher of a day school for pupils with EBD admitted that he had never set foot in another EBD school. This, to us, reflects failings not in the teacher but in the LEA involved. More enlightened authorities would surely agree that staff can only benefit from seeing how other schools operate in terms of behaviour management, curriculum provision, style of teaching, staff deployment and a host of other important variables. All staff, teaching and care, need opportunities to hone their skills and to broaden their practice even if it is essentially sound but all the more so in 'recovering' schools and part of their budget should be devoted to this purpose.

Staff development must also be seen in a broader context. In schools seeking proficiency, as many teachers, RSWs and other support staff as possible need to work from a sound theoretical as well as practical base. Here, specialist, long award-bearing courses seem to be of benefit but, if these cannot be afforded, membership of professional bodies and subscriptions to journals can help 'bring in' the outside world and draw attention to a rich source of ideas. Staff can also benefit from appropriate short courses in a range of subjects offered on or off site.

In addition, as part of each staff member's supervision and appraisal, personal development plans, which identify priority training needs and practical ways of addressing these, seem to be valued in proficient schools. Work-shadowing or team-teaching with 'expert' colleagues can also assist and teachers in our study reported how useful they found visits to mainstream schools to observe practice, to borrow teaching ideas or to view equipment or schemes not previously known to them.

In some of our schools, educational psychologists were used effectively to assist with the development of both teachers and care workers. An increase in practical advice from LEA advisers might also be welcomed and there is clearly potential for counsellors and therapists to help staff to develop skills and lend a sympathetic ear to staff difficulties.

In time, electronic communication could also be used to spread good practice and to provide support to, and to seek advice from, colleagues across the country and indeed across national boundaries. Many special educational needs coordinators (SENCO) now have their own web site. A similar service could soon exist for other workers and video conferencing might give this a more human tinge and increase appeal.

The regional structures recently proposed by DfEE (1997) for special education might assist in the setting up and coordination of new services, and the general monitoring, collation and dissemination of good practice among teachers, RSWs and other staff. Perhaps staff could also be encouraged to set up and run small 'action research' projects. These could be of interest and of practical help to many colleagues in other establishments; many wheels have been reinvented in special schools which better communication could have made unnecessary.

All these approaches can assist in the development of receptive staff but if, after years of debilitating service, senior staff do not have the energy to adjust their ways or to learn from the practice of others, then the more radical step of bringing in new managers is sometimes the only solution. It is noticeable that long-serving senior staff have rarely remained in post for long if their school has been placed in special measures by HMI. There have been occasions when this has seemed very rough justice but it can bring in energetic new blood and it offers schools the chance of radical change.

The 'P's of proficiency increase inclusion

We encountered many pupils in both residential and day schools who appreciated the fresh start that special schooling had given them. Many had been rescued from unhappy situations in the mainstream and found respite, ego-boosting relationships and re-signification outside the mainstream in the ways Cooper (1993) noted. Yet when we observed how these pupils were treated in class and in care situations, we did not see unusual practice happening, other than the fact that they were being taught and cared for in small groups with small pupil/staff ratios which allowed more generous allocation of time to the individual child than would have been possible in the mainstream. The majority of the schools we visited were not characterised by the application of sophisticated theories except in a small number of cases where pupils might have been described as 'beyond EBD', being either seriously delinquent, suffering from severe psychiatric conditions or with pronounced genetic or biological abnormalities. What seemed to take place for the majority of pupils was the application of good basic teacher- and social-pedagogy. Most important was the fact that RSWs appeared as dedicated people willing to make personal sacrifices on children's behalves. They were able, and willing, to form relationships and pay close attention to children's needs and were skilled in using the life-space to support a child's social, emotional and sometimes educational development. Meanwhile, teachers in class provided a structured but forgiving framework which responded to individual need. They offered carefully differentiated work with imagination and conviction. Their style of teaching allowed for frequent positive reinforcement; for pupil participation; for experiential and practical approaches. As some pioneer workers with maladjusted children (see Bridgeland 1971) and as Wilson and Evans (1980), The Elton Report (DES 1989a) and Grimshaw with Berridge (1994) all found and as HMI and OFSTED have more recently advocated, good teaching helps to minimise behavioural difficulties. But, so too, does proficient child care outside the classroom and this is currently not recognised as it should be in the OFSTED framework.

The question then has to be asked, if there is little special about special school practice why do so many children need to go to special schools? Work currently being undertaken by the authors in the mainstream emphasises a further quandary. Why do some schools press for more children to be transferred to special schools for behavioural reasons than other schools who serve apparently similar clientele in terms of range of ability and socio-economic backgrounds? 'Difficult families' and 'difficult estates' lacking social cohesiveness and abounding with anti-school role models, do make life much more difficult for school staff, but why do the OFSTED reports record such differences in schools serving similarly challenging catchment areas?

It is clear that how schools operate does make a difference. If skilled staff existed in greater numbers in schools which have difficult pupils; if they were supported with greater numbers of LSAs and perhaps teachers with professional skills in EBD; if pastoral systems could progress beyond the instruments of social control, identified by Power (1996); if more collaborative styles of teaching and learning could be evolved; if the daily pressures on teachers could be eased to allow them more time to devote attention to all their pupils, there would be then more chance of realising in the mainstream the various 'p's of proficiency described in the first half of this chapter. These would be equally beneficial there to pupils labelled, or in danger of being labelled, as EBD as they are in special schools and the pressure to segregate these pupils would be reduced.

The evidence of our study suggests that proficient schools for pupils with EBD are the 'schools for individuals' desired by Cooper (1993). All children are well known, their affective and cognitive needs understood and education and care programmes are designed accordingly. A holistic view of every pupil is taken and his, or her, attachment to the staff and to the school carefully nurtured. When behavioural challenges are presented it is the sin that is condemned not 'the sinner'. Forgiveness and understanding emanate from staff while negative labelling and the creation of Hargreaves *et al.*'s (1975) 'secondary deviance' thus avoided. Some mainstream schools, particularly those which are subdivided into smaller units to facilitate and strengthen the ties between teachers and pupils to aid the creation of a sense of belonging, also seem to follow these practices – and to good effect with the pupil likely to be labelled EBD.

Our research in the mainstream again suggests the importance of leadership and it has been noted in schools which seem to cope best with children with emotional and behavioural difficulties that the leadership has sometimes had experience of working with pupils with SEN. They possess an empathy for the child; they genuinely value children who are not going to set the world alight with their academic performance. They help to foster whole-school pastoral systems of the sort advised by Galloway (1990). They also seem aware that schools which adopt a holistic approach, tending to the expressive order as well as to the instrumental, often attain better examination results. That which works to the benefit of the child with EBD allows for, and sometimes improves, achievement in examinations for many more pupils. Skilled teachers can expect and attain high standards in their particular subjects while at the same time paying attention to the wider emotional and social needs of their pupils.

The mainstream school has certain advantages: size allows more specialist teaching and a wider range of options which can facilitate the educational 'offer' at Key Stages 3 and 4 if skilled and creative teachers, operating from a similar value base as that described above for SMTs, are given the space and time to evolve programmes, which match the learning styles and needs of children with EBD (Visser 1993).

The conditions described in the preceding paragraphs are difficult to meet. Indeed our hopes for the mainstream might be greeted with a weary smile by stressed SENCOs and senior staff. When one of the authors discussed developing home visiting programmes with the SENCO of an urban comprehensive, she agreed that it would be beneficial but fairly asked how the time was to be found. During the school day she was occupied with frequent 'fire-fighting', clearing up situations precipitated by staff with little empathy for pupils with EBD. Before, and after, the school day she was attending meetings. She did not think she could give any more and there was no one to help her.

It seems essential that mainstream teachers have more help from LEA behaviour support services than is currently the case. They could also benefit from more active involvement of educational welfare officers, social workers, health service professionals and perhaps the police – but these agencies have their own agendas, their own priorities, their own overspent budgets. 'Interagency working is not rocket science, it's more difficult' proclaimed the advertisement for a recent American seminar (Kukic 1997). Yet examples of close working between different professions which result in the lessening of pupils' difficulties do exist and were occasionally seen on our visits. More could be done to keep more children in mainstream settings. Indeed there are children in the mainstream without the label EBD who present more severe challenges to teachers and who have more complicated and stressful home circumstances than some of the pupils we observed in special schools.

Conclusion

We are not utopian. Progress towards greater inclusion for more children presenting behavioural challenges will be slow and uneven but where mainstream schools create the holistic, responsive ethos, develop staff with the skills described in Chapter 4, are given support by other agencies, and the 'p's of proficiency are realised in daily practice, greater inclusion will happen. However, as we stated at the start of this chapter, there will still remain some children with EBD who will only thrive in small, generously staffed special schools where more time can be devoted to their needs. The need for special schools for these pupils will remain.

Progress towards realising high standards consistently in these special schools will not be easy. 'EBD special schools face quite exceptional challenges. Some meet these challenges superbly' (DfEE 1997, p. 86). These words from the 1997 'green paper' on special education deserve far wider publicity than they are likely to receive. They are followed by a recognition, likely to attract more attention, that too many schools show too many weaknesses. It is hoped that the findings of the project reported in this book will assist in making similar comments unnecessary in future government publications.

The University of Birmingham Research Project

The project on which this book is based ran for two years from 1 January 1996. The research team consisted of the Project Director, John Visser; the Research Fellow, Ted Cole and the Chairman of the Steering Group, Professor Graham Upton. Funding was provided by the Shotton Hall Trust. The project's purpose was the identification and dissemination of 'good practice'. An additional goal was the building of a knowledge base on provision for pupils with EBD.

The first task was to compile a comprehensive list of special schools for pupils with EBD. This was undertaken in Spring 1996, by comparing a DfEE list of schools existing on 1 January 1994 for pupils with EBD, entries in national education directories, personal knowledge and advertisements in the specialist press. Schools catering primarily for children with learning difficulties (which were also registered with DfEE as schools catering for pupils with EBD) were excluded from our list.

The second task was to conduct a national survey by a detailed questionnaire (see Appendix 2). A supplementary questionnaire on child care and another on abuse allegations and the Children Act were also distributed. These survey instruments were constructed after a study of the literature and consultation with the Project's Steering Group (see below).

The questionnaires were piloted in April and May 1996, on a small group of serving or former headteachers of schools for pupils with EBD or EBD/MLD and revisions made. The final versions were sent out in late May 1996 to the headteachers of every school for pupils with EBD that we had identified. 'Reminder' questionnaires were sent to schools who had not replied in September and December 1996 and January 1997.

When additional schools were identified as catering primarily for pupils with EBD questionnaires were sent to them. It was not possible to obtain a reliable list of 'registered independent' schools and given openings and closures and re-designation of LEA schools (usually from MLD to EBD but also sometimes from 'school' to 'PRU') it is not claimed that our list was a comprehensive list of all the EBD schools in England. However, it is our belief that at least 95 per cent of all English schools for pupils with EBD were invited to participate in the study.

The main questionnaire was sent to the headteachers of 283 schools as categorised in the Table (a few schools which had been sent the questionnaire were later identified as closed; these do not form part of the total).

		Completed and returned by:	Return rate %
Maintained schools	206	112	54.4
Non-maintained schools	14	9	64.3
Approved Independents	34	19	55.9
Registered Independents	29	16	55.2
Total	283	156	55.1

A few of the returned questionnaires indicated that the respondents' schools were due to close in 1996 or 1997. On the other hand a few advertisements were noted in the *Times Educational Supplement* for new LEA schools about to open.

The questionnaire relating to child care arrangements was sent to any school thought to provide residential facilities (over half the sample). Sixty-six returns were received. Early questions (CQ1–8) explored age, sex, experience, gender and rostering details for staff. Other questions (CQ9–11) covered qualifications and suggestions for training; another (CQ12) arrangements for appraisal and supervision.

Questions CQ14 and 15 replicated Q30 and Q31 in the main questionnaire on approaches to the management and motivation of children. Question CQ16 pursued this topic further while the remaining questions covered absconsion rates, homework arrangements and length of school year.

The third questionnaire related to child protection and responses to the 1989 Children Act. It was sent to all the sample and 130 were returned. Questions CP1–6 explored the number, nature and consequences of allegations by pupils or families against staff of child abuse. Question CP7 sought views on the operation of local child protection procedures; CP8 positive aspects of the 1989 Children Act; CP9 views on Department of Health guidance on physical restraint and the final question (CP10) asked respondents to comment on aspects of the 1989 Children Act regulations and guidance they believed to be in need of revision.

During the course of the project, visits were made to 20 schools for pupils with EBD in England; two residential treatment centres in Denmark and four 'programs' for children with severe emotional disturbance in New England, USA.

The Steering Group

Professor Graham Upton (Chairman), then Pro Vice Chancellor, University of Birmingham, now Vice-Chancellor, Oxford Brookes University.
Owen Booker, Shotton Hall Trust.
Keith Bovair, Headteacher, Durants School, Enfied; representing AWCEBD.
Kathy Bull, HMI.
Harry Daniels, Professor of Special Education and Educational Psychology, University of Birmingham.
Tim Exell, Headteacher, Wendover House School, Wendover; representing National Association of Head Teachers.
Linda King, Headteacher, Elsley School, Battersea; representing NASEN.
Sue Panter, Senior teacher, Sheredes School, Hoddesden; representing AWCEBD.
Steve Rayner, Lecturer, University of Birmingham.
Colin Smith, Senior Lecturer, University of Birmingham.
Judith Wade, Professional Officer, Schools Curriculum Advisory Authority.
Paul Wright, Acting Headteacher, Lower Lea School, Liverpool; representing NASEN.

Appendix 2:

The Main Questionnaire

(This is a compressed version – most answer boxes and spaces have been removed)

THE UNIVERSITY OF BIRMINGHAM
NATIONAL SURVEY OF SPECIAL SCHOOLS FOR PUPILS
WITH EMOTIONAL AND BEHAVIOURAL DIFFICULTIES

BASIC INFORMATION

Q1. School /Address/Status (Maintained/non-maintained/approved under 1993 Education Act', 'finally registered' or 'provisionally registered' independent).

PUPILS

Q2. Please give the number of pupils on your school roll in mid-May 1996 in:

Year 2 or below	Years 3 to 6	Years 7 to 9	Years 10 and 11	Year 12	Totals
(Key Stage One)	*(KS Two)*	*(KS Three)*	*(KS Four)* or above		

(Boys/girls/day/part or full-time boarders)

Q3. Please estimate the percentage of the boys and girls attending your school predominantly because of: Boys   Girls

(a) behavioural difficulties (e.g. aggression, destructiveness, truancy, classroom disruption in previous schools etc.)
(b) emotional difficulties (e.g. anxiety, depression, isolation, phobias)
(c) emotional and behavioural difficulties (both present; neither predominant)
(d) other reasons. Please specify

Q4. Indicate % of your present pupils who have been cautioned or charged by the police for criminal acts:

under 10%   10–25%   26–50%   51–70%   Over 70%

(a) before admission to your school
(b) since admission to your school

Q5.
(i) Please indicate the percentage of pupils presently on the school roll who in your opinion:

have significant learning difficulties not caused by their EBDs	have mild learning difficulties not caused by their EBDs	are of average ability	are of above average ability

169

(ii) Please estimate the achievement levels of pupils **on entry to your school** in the core subjects (*in relation to your perception of national averages*):

	average or above achievement	slight underachievement	significant underachievement	serious underachievement
(a) English				
(b) Maths				
(c) Science				

Q6.
(a) How much say does the Headteacher have in deciding which pupils are admitted to your school?

Very substantial ☐   Some ☐   Little ☐   Almost none ☐

(b) Name up to three types of behaviour which would prompt the Headteacher to:

    (i) oppose admission of potential pupils   (ii) permanently exclude a pupil

Q7. Please estimate the percentage of pupils admitted to your school in recent years who stay on roll for:

(a) less than a month   (b) less than a term   (c) less than a school year
(d) 1 to 2 years   (e) 2 to 3 years   (f) more than 3 years

Q8. What percentage of the pupils presently on your school roll spend a portion of the week in a mainstream school or college?

half day or less   half to one day   one to two days   three days or more

STAFFING and MANAGEMENT

Q9.
(a) Tick appropriate box to indicate how long the senior staff have held their present jobs:

	Up to 1 year	1 to 2 years	2 to 5 years	5 to 10 years	Over 10 years
Headteacher					
Deputy Head					

(b) Of the other teachers at your school how many have worked there for:

Up to 1 year	1 to 2 years	2 to 5 years	Over 5 years

Q10. Please fill in the details on the teachers (including Head and Deputy) at your school [*(c) refers to teachers who have successfully completed long award-bearing courses; (d) asks for aggregate of teaching experience gained at previous and at your schools; for (e) and (f) abbreviate subjects to three letters e.g. 'Eng' for English, 'Fre' for French*]

(a) Full/part-time or peripatetic
(b) Total number of half-day sessions or equivalents taught per week
(c) Further special qualifications? (tick box if 'yes')
(d) Total teaching experience
(e) Subjects taught at present by the teacher (*exclude those occupying minor part of his/her timetable*)
(f) Curriculum subjects in which teacher is professionally qualified or for which substantial training has been undertaken

170

Q11.

(a) How many classroom assistants are employed at your school?

(b) Of these how many work:

(i)   ten half-day teaching sessions a week   (ii)   six to nine half-day sessions a week
(iii) three to five half-day sessions a week   (iv) two or less half-day sessions a week

(c) How many of your classroom assistants have completed relevant training courses?

Q12. Do you have a teacher appraisal system?

(a) Tick box if 'yes'

(b) If yes, how often is each teacher re-appraised

(c) Name up to three people who conduct the appraisals (e.g. 'Headteacher', 'other teacher', 'Educational Psychologist')

(d) Do you believe that your existing appraisal system:

	No	*A little*	*Significantly*	*Very significantly*

(i) aids your teachers' professional development
(ii) aids management to achieve its goals

Q13. Does your school have a system for supporting staff/dealing with work related stress? If yes please comment below *(if your school has a written policy on stress management, please could you send us a copy)*

Q14.

(a) Since September 1993, how many staff have been financed by your school, LEA or governing body to start long, award-bearing SEN or EBD courses?

(b) In the school year 1995/6, how many courses have your teachers attended? *(please exclude the five statutory training days and courses for which teachers themselves have paid)*

(i) day courses   (ii) short courses (two days or more)

(c) Which nationally available long or short courses have members of your staff found particularly useful?

Q15. External support: how much input is there at your school from:

	Little	*Some*	*Regular*	*Extensive*

(a) educational psychologists
(b) psychiatrists
(c) education social worker attached to your school
(d) local authority field social workers
(e) others (please name)

Q16. Rate the quality of the input made by external support staff:

	Poor	*Fair*	*Good*	*Excellent*

(a) educational psychologists
(b) psychiatrists
(c) education social worker attached to your school
(d) local authority field social workers
(e) others (please name)

Q17. What is the usual size of teaching group for the core subjects?

Q18.
(a) Does your school have a school development plan?   Yes/No

(b) What influence has this had on improving your school?   Very little/some/much/profound
(Please send us a copy or synopsis of your school's development plan)

THE EDUCATIONAL CURRICULUM

Q19. Name up to three subjects which you regard as having particular therapeutic value for pupils with EBD:

Q20.
(a) Which subjects outside the National Curriculum are included in your school's timetable?

(i) at Key Stage One (ii) at Key Stage Two (iii) at Key Stage Three (iv) at Key Stage Four

(b) Name up to three of these subjects which you regard as particular strengths of your school:

Q21. How do you respond to the following statements? *(please tick appropriate box)*

	Strongly disagree	Disagree	Agree to some extent	Strongly agree
(a) The majority of this school's teachers accept and support most National Curriculum demands	☐	☐	☐	☐
(b) National Curriculum requirements have helped to improve academic achievement in this school	☐	☐	☐	☐
(c) National Curriculum requirements have made it more difficult to meet pupils' personal and social needs	☐	☐	☐	☐
(d) National Curriculum requirements make it more difficult to manage and motivate our pupils	☐	☐	☐	☐

Q22. How easy/difficult is it to meet the statutory requirements of the National Curriculum and to provide religious education in your school? *(please complete appropriate sections for your school; 'not attempted' only an option for independent schools)*

(i) at Key Stage One

	Easy	Quite Easy	Difficult	Very Difficult	Not Attempted
Maths					
English					
Science					
Design and Technology					
Information Technology					

Geography
History
Art
Music
Physical Education
Religious Education

(ii) at Key Stage Two *[all subjects listed again]*

(iii) at Key Stage Three *[all subjects listed again with Modern Foreign Language added]*

(iv) at Key Stage Four *[subjects listed again except Geography, History, Art and Music]*

* *We are aware that providing Design and Technology (including Information Technology) and a Modern Foreign Language becomes statutory at Key Stage 4 in September 1996; for these three areas, please **estimate** how easy/difficult you think it will be to meet National Curriculum requirements in your school.*

Q23. Name up to three National Curriculum areas (and at which Key Stages) which you feel are generally regarded as strengths of your school:

Q24. Name up to three National Curriculum areas to which pupils at your school have generally shown:
(a) the most positive classroom response
(b) the most negative classroom response
(c) Have the **positive responses** named in 24(a) been *primarily* caused by: *(tick one 'yes' box only for each area)*

	Area 1 *Yes*	*Area 2* *Yes*	*Area 3* *Yes*
(i) stimulating National Curriculum content			
(ii) pupils seeing the relevance of the content to their lives			
(iii) a mixture of (i) and (ii)			
(iv) teacher expertise and confidence in the subject matter			

(d) Have the **negative responses** named in 24(b) been **primarily** caused by: *(tick one 'yes' box only for each area)*

	Area 1 *Yes*	*Area 2* *Yes*	*Area 3* *Yes*
(i) inappropriate National Curriculum content			
(ii) pupils not seeing the relevance of the content to their lives			
(iii) a mixture of (i) and (ii)			
(iv) lack of teacher expertise and confidence in the subject matter			

Q25. How do you assess the value of standard assessment tasks for pupils with EBD?

Q26. Do you have any general comments on the National Curriculum as it relates to your pupils?

MANAGING, MOTIVATING and MEETING NEEDS

Q27.
(a) Suggest up to six factors which best characterise the teaching style of effective teachers of children with EBDs?

(b) Are there particular skills or personality traits which distinguish your teachers from what you regard as good 'mainstream' teachers?

Q28. Are there common factors in many pupils with EBD's *learning style* to which effective teachers must pay careful attention? If yes, please mention them in the box below:

Q29. How important are the following in motivating and managing the majority of pupils with EBDs?

[Tick one box only for each of (a) to (h)]

	Unimportant	Quite important	Important	Very important
(a) Well planned individual educational programmes	☐	☐	☐	☐
(b) Frequent pupil involvement in planning their own learning	☐	☐	☐	☐
(c) Helping pupils 'catch up' in basic language and number skills	☐	☐	☐	☐
(d) Creative work in the arts	☐	☐	☐	☐
(e) Improving pupils' self-image by helping them succeed	☐	☐	☐	☐
(f) Frequent use of information technology in many curriculum areas	☐	☐	☐	☐
(g) Structured personal and social education programme	☐	☐	☐	☐
(h) Wide curricula access through differentiated teaching	☐	☐	☐	☐
(i) Challenging but appropriate curricula expectations	☐	☐	☐	☐
(j) Allowing pupils substantial choice in deciding what they should study	☐	☐	☐	☐
(k) Cross-curricular topic work	☐	☐	☐	☐

Q30. How important are the following in addressing the needs of the majority of pupils in your school?

[Tick one box only for each of (a) to (k)]

	Unimportant	Quite important	Important	Very important
(a) A well-established daily routine	☐	☐	☐	☐
(b) Clear expectations and firm, consistent discipline	☐	☐	☐	☐
(c) Caring, long-lasting relationships between staff and pupils	☐	☐	☐	☐
(d) Regular individual sessions with qualified counsellor/therapist	☐	☐	☐	☐
(e) Touch/holding children by staff to comfort or to ease tantrums	☐	☐	☐	☐
(f) Helping children to express their feelings appropriately	☐	☐	☐	☐

(g) Staff who listen to children
and reflect back their feelings
☐ ☐ ☐ ☐

(h) Group discussions/meetings
with skilled staff
☐ ☐ ☐ ☐

(i) Key-worker or 'named person'
for each pupil
☐ ☐ ☐ ☐

(j) Use of drug therapy *(other
than for the control of epilepsy)*
☐ ☐ ☐ ☐

(k) 'Sorting out' pupil's EBD
before stressing their education
☐ ☐ ☐ ☐

(l) Frequent encouragement and praise
☐ ☐ ☐ ☐

Q31. (i) Tick the 'yes' box if your school has: [and] (ii) rate the usefulness of (a) to (i)

	(i) Yes	*Little use*	*Some use*	*Useful*	*Very useful*
(a) A detailed written behaviour management policy	☐	☐	☐	☐	☐
(b) A behaviour management system based on points or tokens	☐	☐	☐	☐	☐
(c) Children's council/court to discuss misbehaviour	☐	☐	☐	☐	☐
(d) Incentives agreed and applied by all staff	☐	☐	☐	☐	☐
(e) Sanctions/deterrents agreed and applied by all staff	☐	☐	☐	☐	☐
(f) Extra staff to look after pupils wandering/ejected from class	☐	☐	☐	☐	☐
(g) Community meetings where pupils express their views	☐	☐	☐	☐	☐
(h) A complaints procedure clearly understood by pupils	☐	☐	☐	☐	☐
(i) A written, detailed physical restraint policy	☐	☐	☐	☐	☐

Q32. In what ways do the pupils of your school mix with the local community?

Q33.
(a) On average how many (i) teachers sit with the pupils at lunch each weekday
(ii) care or other support staff sit with the pupils at lunch each weekday

(b) What arrangements are made for pupils during weekday playtimes? *(staff/pupil ratios/activities offered etc.?)*

Q34. Are there other effective approaches used by your staff not mentioned or insufficiently stressed in Q29 to Q33 which help to distinguish the special from the mainstream school experience for pupils with EBD?

PARENTS and CARERS

Q35. Links with pupil's families/carers

(a) What reports are sent to parents/carers? *(length, nature and frequency)*
(b) Which members of staff make visits to pupils' homes and how often?
(c) What meetings take place at school to which parents/carers are invited?
(d) Which staff attend case review meetings to which parents/carers are invited e.g. at Social Services offices?
(e) What other means of contact are there between school staff and parents/carers?

Q36. Please rate parents' attitudes to their child's placement at your school; estimate % of parents who are:

　　　　Negative　　　Accepting but cool　　　Favourable　　　Very positive

POLICY IMPACT

Q37.
(a) What is your opinion of local management of special schools? *(tick appropriate box)*

　　　　Negative　　　Accepting but cool　　　Favourable　　　Very positive

(b) How is your school coping with LMSS? *(tick appropriate box)*

　　　　Easily　　　Fairly easily　　　With some difficulty　　　With much difficulty

Q38. If you have been inspected or will shortly be inspected under Ofsted procedures:

(a) Please give the month and year in which the inspection took/is to take place
(b) Please comment on your school's experience of the Ofsted inspection process
(c) To what extent has the Ofsted inspection and report aided the positive development of your school?

　　　　Not at all　　　A little　　　To some extent　　　Substantially

Q39.
(a) Do you feel the long-term future of your school is *(tick appropriate box)*:

　　　　Very insecure　　　Insecure　　　Fairly secure　　　Secure

(b) Are major changes in provision for pupils with EBD being planned or implemented by your LEA (or if you are a non-maintained or independent school, in some of the LEAs who regularly place children at your school)? If 'yes' please mention them here:

Q40.
(a) Has the nature of the pupil intake of your school changed in the last five years? If 'yes', tick box
(b) If 'yes' please indicate in what ways

OUTCOMES

Q41. *(for all-age or junior schools)*

Please give your school's most recent *end of Key Stage Two*

(a) statutory teacher assessments of pupils:

176

(b) standard assessment tasks results:

Q42.
(a) How many pupils have left your school to enter full-time mainstream education in the last three years?
(b) What % of these transfers do you believe to have been

(i) successful   (ii) quite successful   (iii) not very successful
(iv) a failure   (v) unable to judge

Q43. Please give details on your pupils' success in obtaining national qualifications:
(a) Numbers of pupils in 1995:
(i)   gaining 1 or more GCSEs Grades A–G   (ii) gaining 1 or more GCSEs Grade A–C
(iii) gaining 5 or more GCSEs Grade A–G   (iv) gaining 5 or more GCSEs Grade A–C
(b) AEB Basic Skills Exams

(c) City and Guilds

(d) GNVQs

(e) Others

(f) Are there particular courses *(please name awarding body/exam board)* which you would recommend to other schools for children with EBD?

(g) What percentage of pupils who left at 16 years or older in 1995
                (i) entered FE?   (ii) went into full-time employment?

Q44.
(a) Does your school compile a detailed 'Record of Achievement' folder for each pupil? Tick box if 'yes'.
(b) If 'yes', what is the value of the 'Record of Achievement' folder? *(tick appropriate box)*
                                        None   Little   Some   A great deal
(i)   to the majority of your leavers
(ii) to most parents of leavers
(iii) to FE admissions tutors
(iv) to potential employers of the leavers

Q45. What other factors demonstrate the success of your staff in helping your pupils?

CONCLUSION

Q46. Despite the length of this questionnaire you may feel that you have not had the opportunity to describe positive and distinctive features of your work which help to make life for the pupils at your school 'special' and different from the kind of education and care they would be likely to receive in a mainstream school. Please use the space below for this purpose.

References

Aichhorn, A. (1951) *Wayward Youth*. London: Imago.

Ainscow, M. (ed.) (1991) *Effective Schools for All*. London: David Fulton Publishers.

Ainsworth, F. and Fulcher, C. (eds) (1981) *Group Care for Children: Concepts and Issues*. London: Tavistock.

Aldgate, J., Maluccio, A., Reeves, C. (1989) *Adolescents in Foster Families*. London: Batsford.

Allen, B. J. (1998) *Holding Back*. Bristol: Lucky Duck Publishing.

Amos, M. (1997) *Personal communication*, 4 June.

Anderson, E. (1994) *In Loco Parentis: Training Issues in Boarding and Residential Environments*. London: David Fulton Publishers.

Andersen, E. and King, C. (1994) 'The residential environment', in Anderson, E. *In Loco Parentis: Training Issues in Boarding and Residential Environments*, 188–98. London: David Fulton Publishers.

Apter, S. (1982) *Troubled Children, Troubled Systems*. New York: Pergamon.

Argyle, M. (1978) *The Psychology of Interpersonal Behaviour*, 3rd edn. Harmondsworth: Penguin.

ASDAN Bristol Award Scheme Development and Accreditation Network. (1994) Circular to headteachers, October.

Asen, A. (1996) 'Helping the families of problem children', in Varma, V. (ed.) *Managing Children with Problems*, 106–18. London: Cassell.

Association of Workers for Children with EBD (AWCEBD) (1997) 'Consulting, consulting', *Newsletter*, December, 7.

Audit Commission/HMI (1992) *Getting in on the Act: Provision for Pupils with Special Educational Needs*. London: HMSO.

Ayers, H., Clarke. D., Murray, A. (1995) *Perspectives on Behaviour: A Practical Guide to Effective Interventions for Teachers*. London: David Fulton Publishers.

Balbernie, R. (1966) *Residential Work with Children*. Oxford: Pergamon.

Barnes, F. H. and Barnes, L. (1996) 'The convergence of the Israeli and the European experience: implications for group care services in the United States', *Residential Treatment for Children and Youth* 13(3), 49–62.

Barratt, C. J. (1988) 'The location of residential schools for the maladjusted: a case study', *Maladjustment and Therapeutic Education* 6(3), 178–85.

Beedell, C. (1970) *Residential Work with Children*. London: Routledge and Kegan Paul.

Beedell, C. (1993) *Poor Starts, Lost Opportunities, Hopeful Outcomes*. London: Charterhouse Group.

Begg, J. D. (1982) 'The therapeutic community', in McMaster, J. M. (ed.) *Methods in Social and Educational Caring*, 104–17. Aldershot: Gower.

Bernstein, B. (1977) *Class, Codes and Control*, rev. edn. London: Routledge and Kegan Paul.

Berry, J. (1975) *Daily Experience in Residential Life*. Routledge and Kegan Paul.

Bettelheim, B. (1950) *Love is Not Enough*. Glencoe, Illinois: Free Press.

Blatchford, P. and Sharp, S. (1994) *Breaktime and the School: Understanding and Changing Playground Behaviour*. London: Routledge.

Blyth, E. and Milner, J. (eds) (1996) *Exclusion from School*. London: Routledge.

Bowers, T. (1996) 'Putting the "E" back in EBD', *Emotional and Behavioural Difficulties* **1**(1), 8–13.

Bowlby, J. (1953) *Child Care and the Growth of Love*. Harmondsworth: Penguin.

Bradshaw, K. (1997) 'The integration of children with behaviour disorders: a longitudinal study'. Paper presented to Council for Exceptional Children's Annual Convention, Salt Lake City, 10 April 1997.

Brendtro, L. (1969) 'Establishing relationship beachheads', in Trieschman, A., Whittaker, J. K., Brendto, L. *The Other Twenty Three Hours*, 51–99. Chicago: Aldine.

Brennan, W. (1985) *Curriculum for Special Needs*. Milton Keynes: Open University Press.

Bridgeland, M. (1971) *Pioneer Work with Maladjusted Children*. London: Staples.

Bull, K. (1995) 'On common ground', *Special Children* 83, 18–20.

Bush, L. and Hill, T. (1993) 'The right to teach, the right to learn', *British Journal of Special Education* **20**(1), 4–6.

Caring for Children (1996) *Mechanical Surveillance and Allied Techniques*, Policy document. Huddersfield: CFC.

Carlebach, J. (1967) *Caring for Children in Trouble*. London: Routledge and Kegan Paul.

Chaplain, R. and Freeman, A. (1994) *Caring under Pressure*. London: David Fulton Publishers.

Charlton, T. and David, K. (eds) (1993) *Managing Misbehaviour in Schools*. London: Routledge.

Chazan, M., Laing, A., Davies, D. (1994) *Emotional and Behavioural Difficulties in Middle Childhood*. London: Falmer Press.

Clough, R. (ed.) (1997) *Emotionally Troubled Children: Agency Planning and Specialist Resources*. Lancaster: Charterhouse Group and Lancaster University.

Cole, B. E. (1981) *The Use of Residential Education to Improve Pupils' Self-Image*. Unpublished MEd dissertation, University of Newcastle upon Tyne.

Cole, T. (1986) *Residential Special Education: Living and Learning in a Special School*. Milton Keynes: Open University Press.

Cole, T. (1989) *Apart or A Part? Integration and the Growth of British Special Education*. Milton Keynes: Open University Press.

Cole, T. and Visser, J. (1998) 'How should the effectiveness of schools for pupils with EBD be assessed', *Emotional and Behavioural Difficulties* **3**(1), 37–43.

Cooper, P. (1993) *Effective Schools for Disaffected Students*. London: Routledge.

Cooper, P. (ed.) (1995) *Helping Them to Learn*. Stafford: NASEN.

Cooper, P. (1996) 'Giving it a name: the value of descriptive categories in educational approaches to emotional and behavioural difficulties', *Support for Learning* **11**(4), 146–50.

Cooper, P., Smith, C., Upton, G. (1991a) 'Ethnic minority and gender distribution among staff and students in facilities for school students with EBD', *British Journal of Sociology of Education* **12**(1), 77–94.

Cooper, P., Smith, C., Upton, G. (1991b) 'The qualifications and training of workers for pupils with emotional and behaviour difficulties,' *Maladjustment and Therapeutic*

Education **9**(2), 83–7.

Cooper, P., Smith, C., Upton, G. (1994) *Emotional and Behavioural Difficulties*. London: Routledge.

Couzens, B. (1997) Personal communication, 4 July.

Cunningham, C. and Davis, H. (1985) *Working with Parents*. Milton Keynes: Open University Press.

Curry, M. (1997) 'Providing emotional support through Circle Time: a case study', *Support for Learning* **12**(3), 126–29.

Davies, J. D. and Landman, M. (1991) 'The National Curriculum in special schools for pupils with EBDs: a national survey', *Maladjustment and Therapeutic Education* **9**(3), 130–35.

Davies Jones, H. (1986) 'The profession at work in contemporary society', in Courtioux, M. *et al. The Social Pedagogue in Europe – Living with others as a profession*, 74–108. Zurich: Federation Internationale des Communautes Educatives (FICE).

Dawson, R. (1980) *Special Provision for Disturbed Pupils: a Survey*, Schools Council Research Studies. London: Macmillan.

Department for Education (1994a) *Pupil Behaviour and Discipline*, Circular 8/94. London: DfE.

Department for Education (1994b) *The Education of Children with Emotional and Behavioural Difficulties*, Circular 9/94. London: DfE.

Department for Education (1994c) *The Education of Children being Looked After by Local Authorities*, Circular 13/94. London: DfE.

Department for Education (1994d) *Code of Practice on the Identification and Assessment of Special Educational Needs*. London: DfE.

Department for Education and Employment (1996) *Boarding Accommodation: A Design Guide*. Building Bulletin 84. London: HMSO.

Department for Education and Employment (1997) *Excellence for all Children*. Cm 3785. London: HMSO.

Department of Education and Science (1965) *Boarding Schools for Maladjusted Children*, Building Bulletin 27. London: HMSO.

Department of Education and Science (1973) *Staffing of Special Schools and Classes*, Circular 4/73. London: DES.

Department of Education and Science (1974) *The Health of the School Child, 1971–2*. London: HMSO.

Department of Education and Science (1975) *Discovery of Children Requiring Special Education and the Assessment of their Needs*, Circular 2/75. London: DES.

Department of Education and Science (1978a) *Report of the Committee of Enquiry into the Education of Handicapped Children and Young People* (The Warnock Report). London: HMSO.

Department of Education and Science (1978b) *Survey of Special Units for Pupils with Behavioural Problems*, Report by HMI. London: DES.

Department of Education and Science (1978c) *Community Homes with Education*. London: HMSO.

Department of Education and Science (1987) *Good Behaviour and Discipline in Schools*. Report by HMI. London: DES.

Department of Education and Science (1989a) *Discipline in Schools: Report of the Committee of Enquiry chaired by Lord Elton* (The Elton Report). London: HMSO.

Department of Education and Science (1989b) *A Survey of Provision for Pupils with Emotional/Behavioural Difficulties in Maintained Special Schools and Units*, Report by

HMI. London: DES.

Department of Education and Science (1989c) *Special Schools for Pupils with Emotional and Behavioural Disorders*, Circular 23/89. London: DES.

Department of Education and Science (1990) *Staffing for Pupils with Special Educational Needs*, Circular 11/90. London: DES.

Department of Health (1991a) *The Children Act 1989: Guidance and Regulations. Volume 4: Residential Care*. London: HMSO.

Department of Health (1991b) *The Children Act 1989: Guidance and Regulations. Volume 5: Independent Schools*. London: HMSO.

Department of Health (1996) *Taking Care, Taking Control*. London: DoH.

Department of Health and Social Security (1970) *Care and Treatment in a Planned Environment*. Advisory Council on Child Care. London: HMSO.

Dockar-Drysdale, B. (1968) *Therapy in Child Care*. London: Longman.

Dunham, J. (1992) *Stress in Teaching*, 2nd edn. London: Routledge.

Earley, P., Fidler, B., Ouston, J. (eds) (1996) *Improvement Through Inspection?* London: David Fulton Publishers.

Elliott, M. (1991) (ed.) *Bullying: a Practical Guide for Coping for Schools*. Harlow: Longman.

Franklin, M. (1945) *The use and misuse of planned environmental therapy*. London: Psychological and Social Services.

Galloway, D. (1990) *Pupil Welfare and Counselling*. London: Longman.

Galloway, D. and Goodwin, C. (1979) *Educating Slow-Learning and Maladjusted Children: Integration or Segregation?* London: Longman.

Galloway, D. and Goodwin, C. (1987) *The Education of Disturbing Children*. London: Longman.

Garner, P. (1993) 'What disruptive students say about the school curriculum and the way it is taught', *Therapeutic Care and Education* 2(3), 404–15.

Garner, P. and Gains, C. (1996) 'Models of intervention for children with emotional and behavioural difficulties', *Support for Learning* 11(4), 141–45.

Gemal, B. (1993) 'Factors influencing decisions about placement of children with emotional and behavioural difficulties', *Therapeutic Care and Education* 2(2), 295–313.

Gittins, J. (1980) Lecture presented at Newcastle University.

Gouldner, A. (1956) 'Cosmopolitans and locals', *Administrative Quarterly Review*, 2.

Greenhalgh, P. (1994) *Emotional Growth and Learning*. London: Routledge.

Grimshaw, R. (1995) 'Placement and progress in residential special schools for children with emotional and behavioural difficulties', in Farrell, P. (ed.) *Children with Emotional and Behavioural Difficulties*, 73–86. London: Falmer.

Grimshaw, R. with Berridge, D. (1994) *Educating Disruptive Children*. London: National Children's Bureau.

Handy, C. B. (1976) *Understanding Organisations*. Harmondsworth: Penguin.

Hanko, G. (1993) 'The Right to Teach – but what are "Lee Canter's children" learning?'. Letter in *British Journal of Special Education*, 20(2), 71.

Hanko, G. (1995) *Special Needs in Ordinary Classrooms. From Staff Support to Staff Development*, 3rd edn. London: David Fulton Publishers.

Hargreaves, D. (1967) *Social Relations in a Secondary School*. London: Routledge and Kegan Paul.

Hargreaves, D., Hester, S., Mellor, F. (1975) *Deviance in Classrooms*. London: Routledge and Kegan Paul.

Hayden, C. (1997) *Children Excluded from Primary School*. Buckingham: Open University Press.

Heywood, J. (1978) *Children in Care*,3rd edn. London: Routledge and Kegan Paul.

Home Office/Department of Health/Department of Education and Science (1991) *Working Together: A guide to arrangements for inter-agency co-operation for the protection of children from abuse*. London: HMSO.

Howe, T. (1995) 'Former pupils' reflections on residential special provision', in Lloyd-Smith, M. and Davies, J. D. (eds) *On the Margins*, 111–32. Stoke: Trentham.

Hyland, J. (1993) *Yesterday's Answers: Development and Decline of Schools for Young Offenders*. London: Whiting and Birch.

Inner London Education Authority (1985) *Educational Opportunities for All? The Report of the Committee reviewing provision to meet special educational needs* (The Fish Report). London: ILEA.

Jacka, A. (1960) *The Story of the Children's Home*. London: National Children's Home.

Kahan, B. (1994) *Growing Up in Groups*. National Institute for Social Work Research Unit, London: HMSO.

Kerr, J. (ed.) (1968) *Changing the Curriculum*. London: Hodder and Stoughton.

King. J. (1993) 'A father to the fatherless: reflections on three decades at the Caldecott Community', *Therapeutic Care and Education* 2(1), 270–80.

Kolb, D. A. (1984) *Experiential Learning*. New Jersey: Prentice Hall.

Kounin, J. S. (1977) *Discipline and Group Management in Classrooms*. New York: Krieger.

Kukic, S. J. (1997) 'Interagency Collaboration is not Rocket Science . . . it's Harder'. Lecture at Council for Exceptional Children's Annual Convention, Salt Lake City, 12 April 1997.

Kyriacou, C. (1991) *Essential Teaching Skills*. Hemel Hempstead: Simon and Schuster.

Laslett, R. (1977) *Educating Maladjusted Children*. London: Granada.

Laslett, R. (1983) *Changing Perceptions of Maladjusted Children*, 1945–1981. London: AWMC.

Lennhoff, F. G. (ed.) (1968) *Learning to Live*. Shrewsbury: Shotton Hall.

Lovey, J. (1991) 'The dilemma of entering disruptive and disaffected adolescents for external examinations', *Therapeutic Care and Education* 9(2), 75–82.

Lund, R. (1992) 'Towards the establishment of a curriculum model for working with children with EBD', *Therapeutic Care and Education* 1(2), 83–91.

Lund, R. (1997) 'Educating children with emotional and behavioural difficulties', AWCEBD *Newsletter*, 5 May.

MacMillan, D., Gresham, F., Forness, S. (1996) 'Full inclusion: an empirical perspective' *Behavioral Disorders* 21(2), 145–59.

Maier, H. (1981) 'Essential components in treatment environments for children', in Ainsworth, F. and Fulcher, C. (eds.) *Group Care for Children: Concepts and Issues* 19–70. London: Tavistock.

Marchant, S. (1995) 'The essential curriculum for pupils exhibiting emotional and behavioural difficulties', *Therapeutic Care and Education* 4(2), 36–47.

Maslow, A. H. (1943) 'A theory of human motivation', *Psychological Review* 50, 370–96.

Maslow, A. H. (1970) *Motivation and Personality* 2nd edn. New York: Harper Row.

McGavin, H. (1997) 'Reducing truancy is key to cutting crime', *Times Educational Supplement*, 30 May.

McKeon, M. (1997) 'Qualifications for life: are GCSEs the answer?', AWCEBD *Newsletter*, 4 May.

McMaster, J. M. (1982) *Methods in Social and Educational Caring*. Aldershot: Gower.

McNair, H. S. (1968) *A Survey of Children in Residential Schools for the Maladjusted in Scotland*. Edinburgh: Oliver and Boyd.

Merrett, F. (1993) *Encouragement Works Best: Positive Approaches to Classroom Management*. London: David Fulton Publishers.

Millham, S., Bullock, R., Cherrett, P. (1975) *After Grace – Teeth*. London: Chaucer.

Ministry of Education (1946) *Boarding School Provision for Educationally Sub-Normal and Maladjusted Children*, Circular 79.

Ministry of Education (1953) *School Health Service and Handicapped Pupils' Regulations*, SI 1156, pt IIIg. London: HMSO.

Ministry of Education (1955) *Report of the Committee on Maladjusted Children* (The Underwood Report). London: HMSO.

Ministry of Education (1956) *Education of the Handicapped Pupil*, 1945–55, Pamphlet 30. London: HMSO.

Ministry of Education (1960) *Report for 1958 and 1959 of the Chief Medical Officer of Ministry of Education*. London: HMSO.

Montgomery, D. (1989) *Managing Behaviour Problems*. London: Hodder and Stoughton.

Moos, R. H. (1974) *Evaluating Treatment Environments*. London: Wiley.

Morgan, R. (1993) *School Life: Pupils' Views on Boarding*. London: Department of Health.

Mortimore, P. *et al.* (1983) *School Matters*. Wells: Open Books.

Mosley, J. (1991) 'A Circular response to the Elton Report', *Maladjustment and Therapeutic Education* 9(3), 136–39.

Moss, S. Z. (1968) 'How children feel about being placed away from home', in Tod, R. J. N. (ed.) *Disturbed Children*, 28–38. London: Longman.

National Commission for Education (1996) *Success Against the Odds: Effective Schools in Disadvantaged Areas*. London: Routledge.

Nelson, C. and Pearson, C. (1991) *Integrating Services for Children and Youth with Emotional and Behavioural Disorders*. Reston, Virginia: Council for Exceptional Children.

O'Reilly, J. (1996) 'Special schools fail to help needy pupils', *Sunday Times*, 24 November.

OFSTED (1993) *Achieving Good Behaviour in Schools*. London: HMSO.

OFSTED (1995a) *Annual Report of Her Majesty's Chief Inspector of Schools*. London: OFSTED.

OFSTED (1995b) *Guidance on the Inspection of Secondary Schools*. London: HMSO.

OFSTED (1995c) *Guidance on the Inspection of Primary Schools*. London: HMSO.

OFSTED (1995d) *Guidance on the Inspection of Special Schools*. London: HMSO.

OFSTED (1995e) *Pupil Referral Units: The first twelve inspections*. London: OFSTED.

OFSTED (1997) *Standards and Quality in Education, 1995/6, The Annual Report of Her Majesty's Chief Inspector of Schools*. London: HMSO.

Orr, R. (1995) 'A prescription for failure', *Special Children*, September, 24–25.

Osler, A. (1997) 'Drama turns into a crisis for blacks', *Times Educational Supplement*, 10 October.

Parsons, C. (1995) *National Survey of LEAs' Policies and Procedures for the identification of, and provision for, children who are out of school by reason of exclusion or otherwise*. Canterbury: DfE/Canterbury Christ Church College.

Peagam, E. (1995) 'The foolish man built his house upon the sand', *Therapeutic Care and Education* 4(1), 9–16.

183

Pettes, D. E. (1979) *Staff and Student Supervision*. London: George Allen and Unwin.

Polsky, H. (1967) *Cottage Six*. New York: Wiley.

Power, S. (1996) *The Pastoral and the Academic*. London: Cassell.

Rafferty, F. (1997) 'Real maths wins praise', *Times Educational Supplement*, 12 December.

Redl, F. (1966) *When We Deal with Children*. New York: Free Press.

Redl, F. and Wineman, D. (1952) *Controls from Within*. New York: Free Press.

Redl, F. and Wineman, D. (1957) *The Aggressive Child*. New York: Free Press.

Reid, K. (1986) *Disaffection from School*. London: Methuen.

Reinert, H. R. and Huang, A. (1987) *Children in Conflict*. New York: Merrill.

Reynolds, D. and Cuttance, P. (1992) *School Effectiveness: Research, policy and practice*. London: Cassell.

Rogers, P. (1994) *Stress Amongst Staff in Special Schools*. Unpublished MEd dissertation, University of Southampton.

Rose, M. (1990) 'The Peper Harow treatment approach', in Fees, C. (ed.) *Residential Experience*. Birmingham: AWMC, 79–90.

Rutman, B. (1992) 'The non-parent adult as a significant role model', *Therapeutic Care and Education* 1(3), 194–202.

Rutter, M. *et al.* (1979) *Fifteen Thousand Hours*. London: Open Books.

Samuels, M. (1995) 'Meeting the curricular needs of pupils in a residential special school for secondary-aged pupils', in Cooper, P. *Helping Them Learn: Curriculum Entitlement for Children with EBD*, 81–102. Stafford: NASEN.

Sanders, D. and Hendry, L. (1997) *New Perspectives on Disaffection*. London: Cassell.

Scottish Office Education Department (1992) *Using Ethos Indicators in Secondary School Self-Evaluation*. Edinburgh: SOED.

Shaw, O. (1965) *Maladjusted Boys*. London: Allen and Unwin.

Smith, A. (1996) *Accelerated Learning in the Classroom*. Stafford: Network Educational Press.

Smith, A. and Thomas, J. (1993a) 'What's in a name: some problems of description and intervention in work with emotionally disordered children', *Pastoral Care*, 295, 3–7.

Smith, A. and Thomas, J. (1993b) 'The psychological support of children with emotional and behavioural difficulties', *Support for Learning* 8(3), 104–106.

Smith, C. J. and Laslett, R. (1993) *Effective Classroom Management: a Teacher's Guide*. London: Routledge.

Social Services Inspectorate/OFSTED (1995) *Education of Children who are Looked After by Local Authorities*. London: Department of Health.

Stanley, D. (1977) *Northumberland Village Homes; An Historical Perspective*. Unpublished DAES dissertation, University of Newcastle-upon-Tyne.

Stoll, L. (1991) 'School effectiveness in action: supporting growth in schools and classrooms', in Ainscow, M. *Effective Schools for All*, 68–91. London: David Fulton Publishers.

Stoll, L. and Fink. D. (1994) 'School effectiveness and school improvement: voices from the field', *School Effectiveness and School Improvement* 5(2), 147–77.

Stott, D. H. (1974) *The Social Adjustment of Children: Manual of the Bristol Social Adjustment Guides*, 5th edn. London: Hodder and Stoughton.

Studt, E. (1968) 'Therapeutic factors in group living', in Tod, R. J. N. (ed.) *Disturbed Children*, 1–11. London: Longman.

Topping, K. (1983) *Educational Systems for Disruptive Adolescents*. London: Croom Helm.

Trieschman, A., Whittaker, J. K., Brendtro, L. (1969) *The Other Twenty Three Hours.* Chicago: Aldine.

Upton, G. (1992) 'Emotional and behavioural difficulties', in Gulliford, R. and Upton, G. (eds) *Special Educational Needs*, 93–110. London: Routledge.

Upton, G. (1996) 'Emotional and behavioural difficulties', in Upton, G. and Varma, V. (eds) *Stresses in Special Educational Needs Teachers.* Aldershot: Arena.

Vander Ven, K. (1991) 'Residential care, education and treatment in the United States', in Gottesman, M. (ed.) *Residential Child Care: an International Reader*, 275–99. London: Whiting and Birch.

Visser, J. (1993) 'A broad, balanced, relevant and differentiated curriculum', in Visser, J. and Upton, G. (eds) *Special Education in Britain after Warnock*, 1–12. London: David Fulton Publishers.

Visser, J. and Cole, T. (1996) 'An overview of English special school provision for children with EBDs', *Emotional and Behavioural Difficulties* 1(3), 11–16.

Visser, J. and Upton, G. (eds) (1993) *Special Education in Britain after Warnock.* London: David Fulton Publishers.

Visser, J., Cole, T., Pritchard, J. (in press) 'The OFSTED inspections model and schools for pupils with emotional and behavioural difficulties', *Emotional and Behavioural Difficulties.*

Vivian, L. (1994) 'The changing pupil population of schools for pupils with EBD', *Therapeutic Care and Education* 3(3), 218–31.

Ward, L. (1980) 'The social work task in residential care', in Walton, R. G. and Elliott, D. (eds) *Residential Care – a Reader in Current Theory and Practice.* Oxford: Pergamon.

Weaver, A. (1968) *A Survey of the Treatment of Maladjusted Children within the Educational System in England.* Unpublished DPhil dissertation, University of Oxford.

Whittaker, J. K. (1979) *Caring for Troubled Children.* Washington: Jossey Bass.

Whittaker, J. K. (1981) 'Major approaches to residential treatment', in Ainsworth, F. and Fulcher, C. (eds) *Group Care for Children: Concepts and Issues*, 89–127. London: Tavistock.

Wills, D. (1960) *Throw Away Thy Rod.* London: Gollancz.

Wills, D. (1967) *The Hawkspur Experiment*, 2nd edn. London: George Allen and Unwin.

Wills, D. (1970) *A Place Like Home.* London: George Allen and Unwin.

Wills, D. (1971) *Spare the Child.* Harmondsworth: Penguin.

Wilson, M. and Evans, M. (1980) Education of Disturbed Pupils, Schools Council Working Paper 65. London: Methuen.

Index